C000242933

BORDEAUX

TOP EXPERIENCES · LOCAL LIFE

NICOLA WILLIAMS

Contents

Plan Your Trip 4

Jardin Public (p103)
PATRICE COPPEE/GETTY IMAGES ©

COVID-19

We have re-checked every business in this book before publication to ensure that it is still open after the COVID-19 outbreak. However, the economic and social impacts of COVID-19 will continue to be felt long after the outbreak has been contained, and many businesses, services and events referenced in this guide may experience ongoing restrictions. Some businesses may be temporarily closed, have changed their opening hours and services, or require bookings; some will unfortunately have closed their doors permanently. We suggest you check with venues before visiting for the latest information.

Bordeaux's Top Experiences

Taste world-class wines at La Cité du Vin (p116)

Take in rooftop views from Cathédrale St-André (p42)

Admire elegant Place de la Bourse (p46)

Visit history museum extraordinaire Musée d'Aquitaine (p44)

Stop in at pilgrimage site Basilique St-Seurin (p96)

Admire the Flamboyant Gothic Basilique St-Michel (p76)

Get immersed in fine art at Musée des Beaux Arts (p48)

See art in a bunker at La Base Sous-Marine (p118)

Dining Out

Gourmet Bordeaux cooks up excellent dining, often paired with exceptional wine lists featuring plenty of wines from surrounding vineyards. Timeless dining icons mingle with new openings in Saint-Pierre and Saint-Paul's tasty tangle of pedestrian streets. Riverfront restaurants lace quai des Chartrons – it's particularly enchanting at sunset.

Bistros & Neobistros

Eating out in foodie Bordeaux embraces the whole gambit of places to eat – cafes, restaurants, bars etc.

But for regional cuisine à la Bordelaise, cooked up using traditional family recipes or with a revisited twist by a Michelin-starred chef, it is the city's bistros and brasseries that shine.

Bordelaise bistros are typically small, casual restaurants with a short, enticing menu of homemade fare, including timeless classics such as *lamproie à la bordelaise* (eel stew) and *entrecôte à la Bordelaise* (beef steak in red-wine sauce).

Neobistros inject a trendy dose of contemporary design and creativity into the traditional bistro formula, both in interior design and in the kitchen.

Brasseries

Brasseries, a faithful stalwart of every French city, resemble large cafes: they open all day, serve coffee and drinks as well as full meals, and usually have a vast pavement terrace.

Fare tends to be traditional, although since the much-celebrated 2015 arrival of British chef Gordon Ramsay at Brasserie Le Bordeaux (p61), located inside the city's most historic hotel, new life has been breathed into the local brasserie scene.

Best Traditional French

La Tupina Outstanding Bordelais cuisine, with many dishes cooked over an open fire. (Pictured above; p84)

JOEBORG/SHUTTERSTOCK ©

Au Bistrot Locavore, seasonal and hardcore-traditional dining near Capucins market. (p84)

Le Bouchon Bordelais Snail stew is a regional treat at this traditional bistro. (p61)

Le Petit Commerce Classic fish and seafood. (p63)

La Boîte à Huîtres Oyster heaven. (p60)

Best Modern French

Mets Mots Creative, seasonal neobistro cuisine by talented chef Léo Forget in Saint-Seurin. (p104)

Le Davoli Gourmet dining with chef David Grangier in Saint-Pierre. (p62)

Best Weekend Brunch

Au Couvent Backstreet address in Chartrons, oozing vintage charm and creativity. (p129)

Le Monologue The urban-cool brunch address in fashionable Saint-Seurin. (p107)

Magasin Général The original brunch spot on the edgy Rive Droite. (p93)

La Grande Poste Sensational Sunday brunch in a former art deco post office. (p110)

Horace Unbeatable brunch-and-craft coffee combo. (p62)

Lifestyle Blogs

Camille in Bordeaux (www.camilleinbordeaux. fr) Where to eat and drink by a 20-something *city-trotteuse* (city trotter).

Bordeaux Replay (https://bordeaux-replay.fr) Dining trends and nightlife in Bordeaux.

Bar Open

Bordeaux places great importance on drinking – be it tasting excellent vintages in a bar à vin (wine bar), guzzling cacolac (chocolate milk made in Bordeaux since 1954) in a cafe or glugging local Darwin beer in an industrial hangar. Medieval Saint-Pierre teems with atmospheric cafe terraces, as do Chartron's riverside quays.

Aperitifs

No French drinking tradition is as fine or as sacrosanct as the aperitif – the ritual of savouring at leisure a pre-meal drink (lunch or dinner) in good company. Bordeaux's bonanza of sun-drenched pavement terraces were clearly designed with aperitif-quaffing in mind and sipping a flute of sparkling Crémant de Bordeaux or glass of Lillet rosé (a local, pink aromatised wine) is a quintessential Bordeaux experience – to be repeated.

Bars & Clubs

The line between drinking and clubbing is often nonexistent – a cafe that's quiet mid-afternoon might have DJ sets in the evening and dancing later on. One thing is certain though: from traditional neighbourhood cafe-bar to cutting-edge cocktail bar or specialist coffee shop, drinking options abound in student-packed Bordeaux. Bars typically open from 7pm to 1am, clubs from around 10pm to 3am or 4am Thursday to Saturday.

Best Cocktails

Symbiose Exceptional signature cocktails paired with exquisite food. (p131)

Le Point Rouge Pre-club cocktails in a hidden speakeasy on quai du Paladate. (p87)

Cancan Achingly cool speakeasy by Parisian duo Romain and Clément; fashionable retro vibe and outstanding music. (p65)

Le Taquin Waterfront cocktails, albeit with a busy road separating the river-facing terrace from the water. (p87)

Best Specialist Coffee

Café Piha Beans are roasted on-site at this

ALVARO GERMAN VILELA/SHUTTERSTOCK ©

colonial-style coffee shop in Saint-Paul. (p65)

Café Gusco Specialist coffee and lunch by the city's only female roaster and barista. (p107)

Le Monologue Caffeine hits in fashionable Saint-Seurin. (p107)

Koeben Scandinavian drink-dine-shop hybrid: coffee shop, upmarket grocery and design-cool boutique. (p107)

La Pelle Café Where to find decent coffee in the Chartrons district. (p132)

Banana Café The perfect coffee stop pre- or post-Musée d'Aquitaine. (p66)

Best Alfresco Terraces

Night Beach Summertime hipster hobnobbing on the rooftop of Grand Hôtel de Bordeaux. (p64)

L'Apollo Vintage-cool pavement seating on a people-watching square in medieval Bordeaux. (Pictured above; p65)

Utopia One of Saint-Pierre's finest cafe terraces, in a former church. (p65)

Café Gusco Bordeaux's only female roaster offers serious coffee on a village-like square beneath trees. (p107)

Ibaïa Café Seasonal, design-chic drinking on the water's edge. (p133)

Party Hotspots

Mainstream nightclubs congregate on quai du Paladate near the train station. Or join locals afloat at I.Boat (p132), hot spot for DJ sets, live concerts and club nights on a barge in industrial Bacalan.

Treasure Hunt

Be it shopping at the weekly market; in exquisite concept stores selling beautiful gifts for him, her and the home; or in tiny boutiques specialising in spices, wine or ingenious umbrella stands invented in situ for Bordeaux's zillions of bicycles, shopping in this city is seriously fun and varied.

Where to Shop

Europe's longest pedestrian shopping street, rue Ste-Catherine, links place de la Victoire and place de la Comédie; 19th-century shopping arcade **Galerie Bordelaise** (rue de la Porte Dijeaux & rue Ste-Catherine; ⏱hours vary) is nearby. Luxury fashion boutiques lace the Triangle d'Or ('Golden Triangle') formed by cours Georges Clemenceau, cours de l'Intendance and Allées de Tourny. Trendy independent boutiques and design shops are concentrated on rue St-James in the Saint-Pierre quarter and rue Notre-Dame in Chartrons.

Souvenirs

Few cities are as generous in riches to take home as Bordeaux. While not everyone will be able to take home copious amounts of wine – every self-respecting wine shop does ship abroad – there are ample other 'Made in Bordeaux' treats to buy as a souvenir. Food stuffs are an obvious gift, while the city's many boutique-styled concept stores brim with beautifully crafted, locally designed homewares. Accessories by Bordeaux designers – tote bags by Cocrico, jewellery by Camille – are a fashionista favourite.

Best Fashion

Les Sisterettes Fashionable clothes and acessories for women, many by Bordelais or French designers. (p51)

Freep'Show Vintage Vintage fashion with a clear retro tech theme going on. (p69)

Blue Madone Vintage designer fashion for men and women; workshops too. (p69)

Galeries Lafayette Bordeaux's central department

GABRIEL12/SHUTTERSTOCK ©

store, with history to boot. (p71)

Quai des Marques Big-brand fashion and accessories at discounted, outlet prices. (p132)

Best Food & Drink

Marché des Capucins Historic covered food market. (Pictured above; p89)

L'Intendant The finest wine shop in town, with bottles that cost from €7 to €5000. (p68)

Jean d'Alos Boutique cheeses; many regional specialities. (p51)

Chocolaterie Saunion Bourgeois, family-run chocolate maker in business since 1893. (p69)

Cave Briau Join Bordelais buying wine at chateau prices. (p111)

Best Concept Stores

Do You Speak Français? Shop for insanely trendy totes, T-shirts and the like in hip Chartrons. (p133)

Yvonne Beautiful lifestyle space with eatery in front of Basilique St-Michel. (p90)

w.a.n Everything is artisan and made in France at this temple to 'slow design' in medieval Saint-Paul. (p73)

Baaam Local, Bordeaux-made products. (p51)

Archibald & Zoé Stylish fashion and homewares, all 100% made in France. (p72)

Le Goût du Papier Ingenious concept store only selling paper items. (p111)

Top Shopping Tips

○ Take along your own bag or basket when shopping for fresh fruit, veg and other edible goodies at the market.

○ *Les soldes* (sales) are held twice a year: three weeks in January and again in July.

Show Time

Entertainment covers the gamut of genres, from classical opera and ballet in the city's historic theatre to cinema in Bordeaux's groundbreaking Méca and hybrid venues hosting fringe art events and soirées. For zoning reasons, many late-night music and dance venues are northeast of Gare St-Jean along the river, on quai del Paludate.

What's On

Get up on the month's cultural events, concerts and happenings with **Sortir** (http://sortirabordeaux.fr), **Bordeaux Les Sorties** (www.bordeaux.sortir.eu) and **Clubs & Concerts** (www.clubsetconcerts.com), freebie listings mags available at the tourist office.

Theatre & Opera

A night out at the theatre at Bordeaux's landmark Grand Théâtre (pictured above; p67) is as much a Bordeaux rite of passage as sipping a glass of Bordeaux red – and has been since the 18th century when Victor Louis (of Chartres-Cathedral fame) designed the stunning building. Plays, opera and ballets enrich its seasonal repertoire.

Bordeaux Sounds

Bordeaux music is on the up and is contributing some edgy and creative sounds to the French music scene. The city is traditionally known for its fantastic world sounds. Track down live music – rock, rap, blues, jazz, folk, whatever – at least Thursday to Saturday nights in an eclectic range of venues: traditional clubs, barges, pubs, riverside bars, alternative artist workshops, state-of-the-art concert arenas. Classical music lovers gravitate to the Grand Théâtre (p67) or Auditorium (p110).

Best Live Music

La Guinguette Chez Alriq Live music by the river on the Rive Droite. (p93)

Rock School Barbey Rock school and host to up-and-coming French and international indie bands. (p88)

SAATON/SHUTTERSTOCK ©

Le Fiacre Longstanding concert and drinking venue in Saint-Pierre. (p68)

Auditorium Premier concert hall for varied genres including classical, jazz and world music. (p110)

Best Alternative Venues

La Base Sous-Marine Spectacular concerts and music gigs in a WWII submarine bunker. (p118)

Les Vivres de l'Art Summer concerts and cultural soirées in an artists' residency. (p125)

Le Garage Moderne Mechanics' garage by day; enticing cultural venue come dusk. (p125)

La Grande Poste Dynamic cultural centre, stage and

eat-drink-space in an art deco post office in fashionable Saint-Seurin. (p110)

Best Music Albums

Republica (Bengale; 2017) Hypnotic ballads by Bordeaux's favourite electro-pop duo, Bengale.

Pentacles (I am Stramgram; 2017) Folk pop with a distinct Bordelaise spin by

solo artist Vincent Jouffroy, aka I am Stramgram; exceptional in concert.

Mousquetaire #2 (Romain Humeau; 2018) Solo album by the lead singer of classic 1990s Bordelais rock band, Eiffel.

In Between (Génial au Japon; 2017) Bordelaise female duo (aka Blandine Peis and Emeline Marceau); pop rock duo with fantastic instrumentals.

Worth a Trip

Bordeaux's dazzling international-circuit concert venue **Bordeaux Métropole Arena** (www.bordeauxmetropolearena.com; 48-50 ave Jean Alfonséa, Floirac), 5km south of the centre, resembles a shiny white pebble.

Wine Tasting

Be it urban bars à vins (wine bars) or wine routes that tango between chateaux and gold-stone villages in the vast wine-growing area around the city, Bordeaux wine is all-consuming. Bordeaux is one of France's largest producers of top-quality wine and dégustation (tasting) is key to penetrating its intoxicating soul.

Courses & Workshops

Learning about the fruits of a wine culture that harks back to antiquity is an experience to savoured.

Top addresses to do just that are wine school École du Vin de Bordeaux (p58) and La Cité du Vin (p116) whose weekly repertoire includes themed wine-tasting *ateliers* (workshops).

Every Thursday an **Atelier After-Work** (one hour, €18) studies a different aspect of wine (wine and chocolate, wine and tea, wine in the ancient civilisations etc).

From April to September, a multi-sensory workshop in English explores world wine and includes four tastings (one hour, €25). Reservations essential.

Tours

The tourist office (p146) and Espace Information Routes du Vin (p117) inside La Cité du Vin take bookings for dozens of excellent wine tours and cruises: whet your palate with the Bacchus Wine Tour (three hours, €69) on foot around the city.

Half-day and day tours combine wine-tasting with cycling, river cruising and vineyard-to-vineyard motoring in a convertible buggy.

In autumn, you can join in the grape harvest.

Best Resources

Bordeaux Wine Trip (www.bordeauxwinetrip.com) The ultimate planning tool for wine tourism in and around Bordeaux.

New Bordeaux (www.newbordeaux.com) Meet Jane Anson, Bordeaux resident

PHILIP BIRD LRPS CPAGB/SHUTTERSTOCK ©

and the leading authority on Bordeaux wine.

Vins de Bordeaux (www.bordeaux.com) Encyclopaedic resource on tasting, choosing and pairing Bordeaux wine; inspired Wine Tunes playlist too.

Best Wine Pairings

Bar à Vin Indulge in a glass of wine and perfectly paired nibbles at this elegant wine bar, overseen by a monumental Bacchus, god of wine (aka local hero), in stained glass. (p64)

L'Envers du Decors Exquisite bistro food and wine in the heart of tasteful wine town St-Émilion. (p113)

Best Tastings

La Cité du Vin Bordeaux's mothership of wine tasting. (p116)

L'Intendant Saturday morning tastings in the city's finest wine shop. (Pictured above; p68)

École du Vin de Bordeaux Offers tastings and classes for serious students of wine. (p58)

Rustic Vines Magical, guided cycling tours with tastings in Bordeaux and its vineyards. (p58)

Bordeaux Be Boat Explore riverside vineyards and wineries with this bespoke boat service. (p26)

Worth a Trip

Vines grow just 4km south of the centre at **Château Les Carmes Haut Briond** (07 77 38 10 64; www.les-carmes-haut-brion.com; 20 rue des Carmes; 1½ hour guided visit with tasting €30; ⏱ 9.30am-12.30pm & 2-6pm Mon-Sat), with cellars by Philippe Starck. To get here take tram line A to the François Mitterrand stop, then walk 10 minutes.

Festivals & Events

Bordeaux celebrates traditional and modern festivals in true Bordelais style (read: with much food and wine-fuelled merriment). From Mardi Gras' street carnival to the city's marathon, May's La Nuit des Musées when museums stay open late or Autumn's vendange (grape harvest), the city entertains every taste and desire.

Best Food & Wine Festivals

Les Épicurales (www.epicuriales.com) For a fortnight in late May and early June, Allés de Tourny by the Triangle d'Or is transformed into a giant pop-up restaurant. Cookery lessons and demos by top chefs too.

Bordeaux Wine Festival (www.bordeaux-wine-festival.com; pictured above) Four-day wine fest in June with tasting pavilions covering 80 appellations in Bordeaux and the Aquitaine region.

Fête du Vin Nouveau et de la Brocante Hot chestnuts roasted at street stalls and tastings of the year's first wine are highlights of this neighbourhood festival held in the old wine-trading district of Chartrons in October. (p129)

Bordeaux SO Good (www.bordeauxsogood.fr) Two-day event in November celebrating Bordeaux cuisine and epicurean culture: cooking classes, demonstrations, wine pairings, communal banquets and Michelin-starred chef encounters. A foodie must.

Bordeaux Tasting Wine buffs swill, sniff, sip and spit Bordeaux *grands vins* in harmony at this two-day wine fair in Bordeaux's majestic Palais de la Bourse in December.

Best Music Fests

Bordeaux Rock (www.bordeauxrock.com) Five-day rock festival in January; internationally known bands and musicians head the line-up, supported by Bordelais artists.

Festival International des Orgues (www.cathedra.fr) A stunning repertoire of organ concerts take to the stage at Cathédrale St-André during its International Organ Festival in July and August.

Festival Relâche (https://relache.fr) Itinerant, open-air music festival bringing concerts, musical soirées, DJ sets and other after-dark events to different summer-time venues.

Climax Festival (http://climaxfestival.fr) Fantastic live music, cultural events and skateboarding at Darwin during this eco-driven festival in September. Expect lectures on environmental

STEPHANE BIDOUZE/SHUTTERSTOCK ©

and ecological issues, a line-up of international names (electro, hip hop, pop, indie) and some world-class performances.

Best Free Events

Mardi Gras (www.carnaval desdeuxrives.fr) Late February or early March sees the city break out into a mesmerising mirage of traditional street parades, concerts, costume-making workshops and urban dance shows. Track down the carnival after-party on place Pey Berland.

Traversée de Bordeaux à la Nage (http://traversee debordeaux.com) Watch 500 intrepid swimmers dive into the River Garonne from the Left Bank and swim 1.7km to the Rive Droite

(Right Bank) – a tradition since 1939.

Fête Le Fleuve (www. bordeaux-fete-le-fleuve. com) Every two years (odd years) the city celebrates its river, the Garonne, with open-air concerts, dancing, eating, drinking and general all-round merriment. The festival closes with fire-works.

Bastille Day Free fireworks on place de la Bourse to join the country in celebrating the storming of the Bastille in Paris by revolutionaries on 14 July, 1789.

Scènes en Ville Free live concerts by up-and-coming Bordelais pop stars on a summertime stage in front of the Hôtel de Ville (city hall) during the month of August.

Marché de Noël Huddle over a *vin chaud* (mulled wine) and browse stalls sell-ing crafts by local artisans at December's quaint Christmas Market on Allées de Tourny.

Digital Diary

Go to https://www.bordeaux-tourism. co.uk/What-to-see-do/Agenda to consult the regularly updated monthly agenda published online by Bordeaux tourist office.

Art

Art lovers will have a field day in graceful Bordeaux where a bevy of treasures await discovery. The city's main art museum, Musée des Beaux Arts, is the obvious place to start, but factor in plenty more time to explore the city's bevy of thrilling alternative-art venues.

PHILIP BIRD LRPS CPAGB/SHUTTERSTOCK ©

Museums & Galleries

Bordeaux's artistic offerings vary from traditional fine-arts exhibits in 18th-century mansions to contemporary shows inside any available space: chateau, colonial warehouse, mechanics' garage. Admission ranges from free to €5 per adult and temporary exhibitions often incur an extra fee. Watch for late- or all-night openings during La Nuit des Musées (https://nuitdesmusees.culturecommunication.gouv.fr) in May.

Street Art

Urban art is alive and well in uber-cool Bordeaux, where street artists find expression in the funky wall murals of the Chartrons neighbourhood. Le M.U.R. is a 35-sq-m wall, first stencilled by celebrity French stencil artist Jef Aérosol in 2014, and painted over with an eye-catching new work each month. Jean-Luc Feugeas is a local Bordelais street artist to look out for; the tourist office (p146) organises street-art walking tours (in French).

Festivals

The Bordelais celebrate their rich art legacy with a bunch of annual festivals, creating the chance to view and experience both new works of art and permanent show pieces. October's **Festival International des Arts** (FAB; http://fab.festivalbordeaux.com) is a key diary date. Each September dozens of street and graffiti artists perform live for three days at **Shake Well** (https://shakewellfest.com).

Miroir d'Eau, designed by Michel Corajoud and Pierre Gangnet, Jean Max et Stéphane Llorca (JML)

Best Period Art

Musée des Beaux Arts
Trace occidental art from the Renaissance to mid-20th century at the city's Fine Arts Museum. (p48)

Musée des Arts Décoratifs et du Design Pottery, porcelain, gold, iron, glasswork and other decorative arts in an 18th-century *hôtel particulier*. (p57)

Best Contemporary Art

Musée d'Art Contemporain Fantastic contemporary art in an 1824 warehouse once used to store French colonial produce. (p124)

Institut Culturel Bernard Magrez Contemporary art

meets 19th-century chateau architecture at this inspired arts centre. (p101)

Le 101 Meet and admire the work of a talented graphic designer in his Chartrons *atelier* (studio) on rue Notre Dame. (p135)

Best Alternative Art

Les Vivres de l'Art Meet today's artists at this fringe art incubator. (p125)

La Base Sous-Marin Contemporary-art exhibitions and 'performances' in a WWII bunker. (p118)

Miroir d'Eau Interactive art at its best: cooling off barefoot in atmospheric mists generated by the world's largest reflective pool. (p56)

Museum Admission Pass

Admission to all the city's mainstream art museums are covered by the **Bordeaux Métropole City Pass** (www.bordeauxcity pass.com; 24/48/72 hours €29/39/46).

Architecture

Bordeaux boasts an exceptional architectural heritage, with gems covering the full gambit of history, from ancient necropolis ruins in the Roman castrum to futuristic millennial gems by the water. As every understandably proud, appreciative Bordelais would typically say, c'est gavé bien (it's really good/cool)!

In a Nutshell

The city's architectural story begins in Saint-Seurin where Gallo- Romans buried their dead in a vast necropolis, and later built an evocative amphitheatre. Architects in the Middle Ages designed some of Bordeaux's most iconic buildings – churches mainly, and walls to protect the growing city. In the 18th century, urban planners demolished Saint-Pierre's rabbit warren of dark, narrow streets to create today's elegant, *belle* Bordeaux.

Unesco World Heritage

The once-black, limestone facades of 18th-century Bordeaux gleamed cream again after a scrub-and-polish in the 1990s. In 2007 the city centre became a Unesco World Heritage site. Bordeaux, after Paris, now boasts more protected buildings than any other French city. Its nickname, Port de la Lune (Port of the Moon), comes from the gentle moon-like curve of the Garonne River that creates its natural harbour.

In the Future

The future lies on the riverbanks where contemporary architects are beavering away on dazzling glass-and-steel office towers, eco-smart skyscrapers and eye-popping new buildings in the brand new neighbourhood of Euratlantique. The glass arch of arts centre La Méca (2019) and the city's new Marine and Maritime Museum – resembling a seven-storey ocean liner by local architect Olivier Brochet – are emblematic of tomorrow's architecture.

SARANYA33/SHUTTERSTOCK © ARCHITECTS CHRISTOPHE CHERON AND CHARLES & THOMAS LAVIGNE

Best Medieval

Basilique St-Seurin Serene beauty and archaeological treasures in a Romanesque basilica. (p96)

Cathédrale St-André A riot of Flamboyant Gothic architecture, with 15th-century bell tower. (p42)

Basilique St-Michel Imposing Flamboyant Gothic church in St-Michel. (p76)

Porte Cailhau Time-travel to medieval Bordeaux with this grandiose, riverfront city gate from the 15th century. (p56)

Best Contemporary

La Cité du Vin Bordeaux icon, crafted as a curvaceous wine decanter. (p116)

Pont Jacques Chaban-Delmas Europe's highest lift bridge shines green and blue at night. (Pictured above; p127)

Bordeaux Métropole Arena Curvaceous white 'pebble' by French architect Rudy Ricciotti. (p17)

Musée de la Mer et de la Marine Ocean-liner of a museum by the Bassins à Flot. (p126)

La Méca Bordeaux's newest kid on the futuristic block.

Best Renaissance

Place de la Bourse Bordeaux's showpiece square, best at sunset. (p46)

Pavé des Chartrons Lineup of *hôtels particuliers* built for wealthy wine merchants. (p126)

Hôtel Ragueneau Wisteriadraped, Renaissance mansion (p53).

History In Situ

Archeological exhibits, scale models and other exhibits inside the fascinating Musée d'Aquitaine (p44) provide an evocative account of Bordelais architecture through the ages.

Active Bordeaux

Be it jogging along the waterfront, popping an ollie or flip-kick with other riders at skateparks in Chartrons and Rive Droite's Hangar Darwin, taking a cooking class or catching the next big (artificial) wave in an indoor surf café, Bordeaux urbanites are an active lot and make the most of their enviable, riverside environment.

River Cruising

View the city from a different perspective: afloat on the Garonne. The tourist office has information on river cruises, including a 1½ hour cruise on the *Aquitania* riverboat (adult/child €15/2) and more elaborate lunch or dinner cruises (adult/child €55/35). Or save cents and simply cruise along the river aboard the city's fleet of B³ river boats run by public transport company TMB.

For an alternative, more intimate river cruise, you can also hop aboard a 12-person boat inspired by the small but nippy barges used by Arcachon oyster farmers to access their beds with **Bordeaux Be Boat** (☎ 05 47 74 41 25; www. bordeauxbeboat.fr).

Cycling

Urban two-wheeling is big in Bordeaux and is as much a way of getting from A to B as a pleasurable leisure activity. The city's bike-sharing scheme run by public transport company TBM (www.infotbm. com) makes it easy to grab a set of wheels and go, and the tourist office has information on cycling itineraries in the city, including an 8km or 34km riverside loop along both banks of the Garonne (pictured above).

Best Outdoor Capers

Miroir d'Eau Splashing around barefoot in the cooling water of Bordeaux's iconic reflecting pool is a Bordeaux essential. Not just for kids! (p56)

Skate Parc des Chartrons Riverside skate park. (p128)

Bordeaux Be Boat River cruises to wineries and

EO NAYA/SHUTTERSTOCK ©

other sites inaccessible to larger boats. (p26)

Promenade des Remparts Urban strolling beneath centurion plane trees, unusually in a small park cladding a short remaining section of the old city walls. (p83)

Jardin Public Botanical garden and 18th-century park. (p103)

Best Indoor Activities

Piscine Judaïque Swimming in an art deco pool from 1936. (p102)

Wave Surf Café Catch the next big wave at this indoor surf cafe in Chartrons. (p127)

Hangar Darwin Urban-cool skateboarding venue in an old hangar. (p93)

Serendipity Craft workshops (origami, candle-making, sewing, flower arranging etc) in one of the city's most stylish concept stores. (p69)

Le Goût du Papier Craft workshops, always with a paper theme. (p111)

CAP Sciences Themed activity workshops: astronomy, film-making, green chemistry, photography and culinary experiments in the Labo Miam; reserve in advance online. (p127)

Bordeaux on Two Wheels

○ Le Garage Moderne (p125) in Chartrons is the place to repair bikes.

○ Rustic Vines (p58) and the tourist office (p146) organise fantastic guided bike rides.

For Kids

RUSSIESEO/GETTY IMAGES ©

With its seemingly endless riverside quays and treasure chest of towers to climb and museums to explore, Bordeaux is a superb city to explore en famille. Be it energy-burning tots or tech-smart teens, all ages are well catered for.

Activities

Cycling is big, with safe, silky smooth cycling lanes skirting the riverfront and elsewhere. **Pierre qui Roule** (www.pierre quiroule.fr) rents bikes for all ages as well as inline skates. For teens, consider a nippy scoot around town on a *trottinette electrique* (electric scooter). Skateboarding is Bordeaux's other much-loved activity for all ages.

Sightseeing

Many museums offer free admission to under 18s; otherwise, children pay roughly up to half price.

Dining Out

Children's *menus* (fixed meals at a set price) are common, but the ubiquitous *steak haché* (beef burger) and *frites* (fries) soon tires. Don't be shy in asking for a half-portion of an adult main – restaurants generally oblige. Fave Bordeaux-kid snacks, typically enjoyed mid-afternoon for *goûter* (tea-time), include a hot dog from Woof (p60) or sweet *chocolatine* (the Bordeaux version of the classic *pain au chocolat*) from any self-respecting bakery in town.

Best for Kids

Tour Pey Berland Climbing the bell tower of the city cathedral is a perfect energy burner. (Pictured above; p56)

CAP Sciences Robotics, digital art, astronomy: top exhibitions and workshops at Bordeaux's science museum (3-18yrs). (p127)

La Cité du Vin Kids get their own 'digital companion' to tour the interactive world of wine; visits end with organic grape juice (+8yrs). (p116)

Wave Surf Café Ride artificial waves (from 8yrs); trampolines too. (p127)

Under the Radar Bordeaux

When Bordeaux's blockbuster museums, monuments and sights begin to tire, the thriving and dynamic metropolis squirrels away an endless stash of unexpected curiosities, less-trodden neighbourhoods and alternative experiences – well away from the tourist trail.

SVETLANA USOLTSEVA/SHUTTERSTOCK ©

Alternative Art

3D neighbourhood maps Admire intricately detailed, 3D maps sculpted in bronze by local artist François Didier in front of La Cité du Vin on quai de Bacalan, place Pey-Berland, place de la Comédie and place du Palais.

Rado (www.facebook.com/rado.bdx) Catch street art and edgy, finger-on-the-pulse artistic projects and happenings at this new space dedicated to 'emerging cultures' in Bassins à Flot.

Arc-en-Ciel (127 ave Émile-Counord) Be dazzled (literally) by Bernard Buhler's curvilinear 'Rainbow' building, a brilliant piece of modern Bordelais architecture in the unexplored Grand Parc 'hood.

Wild Green Spaces

Parc Floral Uncover 96 grape varieties from wild vines sourced worldwide, 500 rose varieties, peonies (May), wild orchids and irises (April, May) in this protected ecological reserve in the north of the city.

Bois de Bordeaux Enjoy 6km of footpaths in 130 hectares of pristine woodland, planted in the 1970s next to an artificial lake. Spot European pond turtles, purple herons and red-backed shrikes.

Placette Billaudel (between rues Billaudel, Fieffé et Françin) The city's first 'urban micro-forest', planted with 500 oak, maple and wild fruit saplings as part of the Bordeaux Grandeur Nature project, begs a Zen moment.

Surprise Wine

Indulge in superb blind tastings at **Blind** (https://blind-bordeaux.eatbu.com), where diners take their pick of contemporary southwest and Pays Basque dishes on the menu and leave creative sommeliers to choose the organic or biodynamic wine.

LGBTIQ+

SAMANTHAINALAOHLSEN/SHUTTERSTOCK ©

Laissez-faire perfectly sums up France's liberal attitude towards homosexuality and people's private lives in general; in part because of a long tradition of public tolerance towards unconventional lifestyles. Bordeaux, being the busy student city it is, enjoys an active gay and lesbian scene.

Bare Essentials

As is the case in almost every French city, Bordeaux's lesbian scene is less public than its gay male counterpart and is centred mainly on women's cafes and bars.

Attitudes towards homosexuality tend to be more conservative in the wine-producing villages – countryside essentially.

Same-sex marriage has been legal in France since 2013.

Pride March

Thousands gather in June to celebrate the city's Pride festival – this annual party has been running since 1996. The opening **Marche des Fiertés** sees 6000 participants march, sing and dance from place de la République to place de la Victoire. Then, in the Pride Village, the real party kicks off!

Best Resources

Wake Up! (www.asso wakeup.org) Bordeaux-based association for gay, lesbian, bisexual and transgender students; first-class source of info on where to go to and what to do.

Cité d'Elles (www.citedelles. fr) Local resource for lesbians: organised hikes, bike rides, coffee hangouts.

LGBTIQ+ Hub

In the heart of Saint-Paul, **Le Girofard** (www.le-girofard.org) is the dynamic LGBTIQ+ centre for the Aquitaine region and the primary meeting spot, info source and hub for gay, lesbian, bisexual and transgender visitors to Bordeaux.

Markets

There's no more authentic way to enjoy a seasonal taste of Bordeaux and rub shoulders with locals than at the market. Springtime, when food markets burst with produce and newfound colour – baby carrots and asparagus, strawberries, pink rhubarb and raspberries – is particularly lovely.

GABRIEL12/SHUTTERSTOCK ©

Market Tradition

Bordeaux has a strong market tradition. Locals have flocked to its premier food market, nicknamed *'la ventre de Bordeaux'* (the belly of Bordeaux) in Capucins since the 14th century to shop for weekly staples. *Brocantes* (open-air antique and flea markets) are a highlight of Saint-Michel.

Best Markets

Marché des Capucins Premier covered food market, around for eons. (p89)

Brocante du Dimanche Antiques, vintage curiosities and cheap bric-a-brac at St-Michel's Sunday-morning flea market. (p90)

Marché des Bouquinistes Weekly secondhand book market on place de la Victoire. (p91)

Les Halles de Bacalan Precisely how a modern-day food market should be. (p128)

Passage St-Michel Covered flea market. (Pictured above; p90)

Best Market Eats

Chez Jean-Mi Sublime market address for oysters and seafood. (p83)

Familia Hybrid brasserie, cafe and restaurant fuelled with produce from adjoining Les Halles de Bacalan. (p131)

Foire de Printemps

Springtime is welcomed with a vast pop-up flea market filling Esplanade des Quinconces for two weeks in April during the annual Foire de Printemps. Over the fortnight enjoy al fresco concerts, tastings and much market madness.

Four Perfect Days

Day 1

Begin with a bird's-eye city view atop **Tour Pey Berland** (pictured above; p56), the fancy belfry of **Cathédrale St-André** (p42). Delve into the cathedral interior, then walk to the **Musée des Beaux Arts** (p48) for a garden lounge and art works by Bordelais artists.

After lunch immerse yourself in Bordeaux's ancient past at **Basilique St-Seurin** (p96) and its **Archaeological Site** (p101). Visit **Palais Gallien** (p102), followed by a late-afternoon mooch amid urban nature in nearby city park, **Jardin Public** (p103).

Come dusk, a post-dinner drink at **Night Beach** (p64) – the chic rooftop bar of landmark Grand Hôtel de Bordeaux – is a Bordeaux rite of passage.

Day 2

CORENTIN/SHUTTERSTOCK ©

Begin on leafy Esplanade des Quinconces: pop into **L'Intendant** (p68) to admire its wine stash. Window-shop in the boutique-rich Triangle d'Or.

In the afternoon, walk north to **Pavé des Chartrons** (p126), lined with luxuriant 18th-century townhouses. Continue north along rue Notre Dame, dipping into its small boutiques and artist workshops en route. Visit the **Musée du Vin et du Négoce** (p124) and/or the **Musée d'Art Contemporain** (p124). End with a two-hour visit at least of Bordeaux's flagship museum, **La Cité du Vin** (p116).

Enjoy dinner and cocktails at **Symbiose** (p131), followed by dancing to live music or a DJ set afloat a decommissioned barge at **I.Boat** (pictured above; p132).

Day 3

PAUL PRESCOTT/SHUTTERSTOCK ©

Day 4

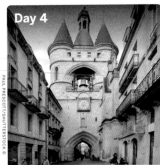

Assuming it's not Monday (when the market is closed), hit **Marché des Capucins** (pictured above; p89) for a breakfast of freshly shucked oysters and white wine at **Chez Jean-Mi** (p83). Meander between stalls heaving with local produce.

In the afternoon enjoy a contemplative visit of **Basilique St-Michel** (p76) and an invigorating hike up its bell tower. Meander south to unsung **Église Ste-Croix** (p82), with exquisite sculpted Romanesque facade and cafe terraces basking in the afternoon sun.

Dine à la Bordelais at **La Tupina** (p84), followed by cocktails at **Le Point Rouge** (p87) and dancing at **La Plage** (p89).

Waltz though Bordeaux history at the **Musée d'Aquitaine** (p44), then continue north to admire Saint-Paul's **Grosse Cloche** (pictured above; p56). Boutique-hop along fashionable rue St-James and people-watch on place Fernand Lafargue.

Explore Saint-Pierre, not missing **Porte Cailhau** (p56) and **Église St-Pierre** (p57). Grab an ice cream at **La Maison du Glacier** (p62) and learn about French customs in the **Musée National des Douane** (p47). Frolic in the mist jets and snap reflections at the **Miroir d'Eau** (p56).

It's a Right Bank evening: sip local craft beer at **Magasin Général** (p93) and dance on the riverbank at **La Guinguette Chez Alriq** (p93).

Need to Know

For detailed information, see Survival Guide p141

Population
250,776

Currency
Euro (€)

Language
French

Money
ATMs at the airport, train station and on every second street corner. Visa, MasterCard and Amex widely accepted.

Mobile Phones
European and Australian phones work, but for American cells only those with 900 and 1800 MHz networks are compatible; check with your provider before leaving home. Use a French SIM card to call with a cheaper French number.

Time
Central European Time (GMT/UTC plus one hour)

Daily Budget

Budget: Less than €140

Dorm bed: €25

Double room in a budget hotel: €80

Admission to many attractions first Sunday of month: free

Lunch *menus* (set meals): less than €20

Midrange: €140–220

Double room in a midrange hotel: €120–180

Lunch *menus* in gourmet restaurants: €20–40

Glass of wine: €3.50–15

Top end: More than €220

Double room in a top-end hotel: €180–350

Craft cocktail in a cocktail bar: €15

Ticket to the opera: €6–110

Top restaurant dinner: *menu* €65, à la carte €100–150

Advance Planning

Three months before Book accommodation, tickets for ballet or opera at Bordeaux's Grand Théâtre, and a table at gastronomic Michelin-starred restaurants if so desired.

Three weeks before In high season, book guided visits and tours organised by the tourist office, particularly wine-tasting workshops and vineyard capers.

Three days before Reserve tables for weekend dinners and meals at Bordeaux's most sought-out dining addresses.

Arriving in Bordeaux

✈ Aéroport de Bordeaux

Also known as Bordeaux-Mérignac, the city's only airport is 10km west of the city centre in the suburb of Mérignac.

Buses run to the city centre and train station (€1.60 or €8) every 30 minutes between 6am to 11pm; the 40-minute journey can be longer in rush hour. Expect to pay €50 for a taxi to the centre.

🚉 Gare St-Jean

Bordeaux's train station, just six hours from London by Eurostar (www.eurostar.com) with a change of train in Paris, retains much of its original grandeur from 1855.

From in front of the train station, bus line 1 runs to place de la Victoire. Tram line C runs north along the river to public transport hub Esplanade des Quinconces (€1.60).

Getting Around

🚌 Bus & Tram

Excellent, reliable transport throughout the city between 5am and 1am. Single tickets (€1.70) are sold onboard buses, from machines at tram stops and online; validate your ticket upon boarding.

🚲 Bicycle

Bordeaux's efficient bike-sharing scheme, V^3, is made for pleasurable cruising for getting from A to B. Initially register online or with your credit card at a V^3 station.

⚓ River Boat

Shuttle boats on the river require a regular bus or tram ticket; regular sailings between 8.30am and 7pm.

🚗 Car & Motocycle

Best avoided. Traffic is often congested and city parking can be frustratingly hard to find.

Bordeaux Neighbourhoods

Saint-Seurin & Fondaudège (p95)
Roman ruins and a winemaker's chateau are highlights of this brilliantly bourgeois area, crafted by rich 18th-century merchants and industrialists.

Basilique St-Seurin

Place de la Bourse

Musée des Beaux Arts

Cathédrale St-André

Musée d'Aquitaine

Basilique St-Michel

La Base
Sous-
Marine

La Cité
du Vin

**Chartrons, Bassins à
Flot & Bacalan (p115)**
Check the pulse of
millennial Bordeaux
in this bohemian
neighbourhood.

**Saint-Pierre, Saint-
Paul & the Triangle
d'Or (p41)**
The city's sightseeing
hub and historic heart,
medieval Saint-Paul and
Saint-Pierre bristle with
ancient churches, cafes
and boutiques.

**Saint-Michel &
Capucins-Victoire
(p75)**
Locals gravitate to this
ethnic 'hood with open-
air antique markets and
the city's premier food
market right next door.

Explore
Bordeaux

View over Bordeaux MARCOCIANNAREL/SHUTTERSTOCK ©

Explore ◉
Saint-Pierre,
Saint-Paul &
the Triangle d'Or

Delve into Bordeaux's ancient heart, a labyrinth of medieval streets named after 13th-century candlestick makers, goldsmiths, coopers and other craftspeople who worked here. North of Saint-Pierre, boulevards lined with elegant townhouses around Esplanade des Quinconces and the chic Triangle d'Or plunge visitors into aristocratic 18th-century Bordeaux.

For a city panorama, hike up the belfry (p56) of Cathédrale St-André (p42). By the river, architecture lovers flock to place de la Bourse (p46) and the world's largest reflecting pool (p56). End the morning with Bordelais history at the Musée d'Aquitaine (p44) or art at the Musée des Beaux Arts (p48). Lunch at Le Bouchon Bordelais (p61). Shop in the afternoon on rue Ste-Catherine and the Triangle d'Or. End with a drink in Saint-Paul.

Getting There & Around

🚌 **Bus** From Gare St-Jean take bus No 1 to place de la Victoire, then walk 10 minutes along cours Pasteur to the cathedral ensemble on place Jean Moulin.

🚊 **Tram** Tram line C northbound from Gare St-Jean or southbound from Esplanade des Quinconces to the place de la Bourse stop on the riverfront; line A east from the Rive Droite to place du Palais.

Neighbourhood Map on p54

Place de la Bourse (p46) ROSSHELEN/SHUTTERSTOCK ©

Top Experience 📷

Take in Rooftop Views from Cathédrale St-André

Bordeaux's Flamboyant Gothic cathedral, with its freestanding belfry crowned by a glittering gold statue of Our Lady of Aquitaine, stands bold and grand. The oldest section dates from 1096 and it was a key stop for medieval pilgrims on the Way of St-James to Santiago de Compostela in Spain. Most of what you see today dates back to the 13th and 14th centuries.

◉ MAP P54, B6

📞 05 56 44 67 29

www.cathedrale
-bordeaux.fr

place Jean Moulin

admission free

🕐 2-7pm Mon, 10am-noon & 2-6pm Tue-Sun

Interior

It was only during the 13th and 14th centuries that the bulk of the cathedral was achieved: the impressive vaulted nave, the choir and ambulatory chapels, not to mention the breaking through of several portals to access this magnificent interior. Behind the altar, in the **Chapelle Ste-Anne**, admire the faint remnants of medieval frescoes on the walls. Glittering stained glass by French master Joseph Villiet (1823–77) casts a magical light over the **Chapelle du Mont Carmel**; the long-lost medieval frescoes here were painted over in the 1860s. Don't miss the organ (1877) and pulpit, richly crafted in mahogany with red marble panels by 18th-century Bordeaux craftsperson Barthélémy Cabirol (1737–86).

Portals

Visitors enter the cathedral through the **Portail Nord** (North Portal), or Portail des Flèches, built between 1330 and 1340. But it is the neighbouring **Portail Royal** (Royal Portal), accessed today from inside the church, that is the stone-masonry masterpiece. It illustrates the Last Judgement according to St-Matthew. When it was built in the mid-13th century the intricate scenes were polychrome painted for 'easy reading,' but recent restoration work has returned the portal to bare, gleaming-gold ochre. This was the only portal not destroyed during the French Revolution (1789) which saw the cathedral transformed into a warehouse storing animal feed.

The Bell Tower

Hike up the 231 steps of Tour Pey Berland (p56), the cathedral's freestanding bell tower built between 1440 and 1466 in a Flamboyant Gothic style.

★ Top Tips

o In summer, catch an occasional *son et lumière* (sound-and-light show) projected on the cathedral façade after dark.

o The cathedral hosts splendid sacred music concerts; buy tickets (€15 or €12 online) at www.cathedra.fr. It's also a memorable concert venue for Bordeaux's annual baroque music festival in June/July and July's Summer Organ Festival.

✕ Take a Break

Grab a seriously good coffee at **Black List** (☑ 06 89 91 82 65; www.facebook.com/blacklistcafe; 27 place Pey Berland; ☺ 8am-6pm Mon-Fri, 9.30am-6pm Sat), across the street from the bell tower. Or hit one of the traditional cafe pavement terraces on the northern side of the cathedral square.

Join locals to enjoy breakfast pre-cathedral or lunch post-cathedral at stylish Horace (p62), a five-minute walk away.

Top Experience 📷
Visit History Museum Extraordinaire
Musée d'Aquitaine

Bordeaux's captivating history and civilisations museum is inside the university's former arts and science faculty. Its permanent collection spans urban history from Gallo-Roman times to 18th-century Atlantic trade and slavery, and the emergence of Bordeaux as a world port in the 19th century. Dynamic and well-curated exhibits are fascinating for all ages.

◎ MAP P54, C8

☏ 05 56 01 51 00

www.musee-aquitaine
-bordeaux.fr

20 cours Pasteur

adult/child €5/free

🕐 11am-6pm Tue-Sun

Antiquity to Middle Ages

The first ground-floor rooms evoke prehistory and archaeological digs in the neighbouring Dordogne executed by high-profile Bordeaux university professors and early explorers. Subsequent rooms recreate the Roman forum (between place de la Comédie and cours de l'Intendance) and floor mosaics found in Roman houses. Don't miss the glass maquette of the Roman amphitheatre, aka Palais Gallien (p102).

Modern Era

Sweeping up the staircase to the upper floor, exhibits move into 18th-century Bordeaux and its pivotal role in transatlantic trade. The museum makes no bones about the 480 'triangle' slave expeditions organised from Bordeaux in the 18th century during which 130,000 to 150,000 African people were purchased in exchange for items such as fabrics and weapons; they were later sold as slaves in the Americas. The logbook of the slave ship *La Licorne* is not a pretty read.

History: Bordeaux's Booming Trade

In the 17th and 18th centuries Bordeaux was a thriving commercial port. Trade was initially two-way: merchant ships laden with Bordeaux wine, oil, flour, silks and other local products sailed to the West Indies and Caribbean, returning with coffee, cocoa, cotton, indigo, spices, sugar and tobacco. But all too soon, the commercial temptations of triangular trade proved too lucrative to resist. Merchandise from all over Europe was shipped from Bordeaux to ports on the East African coast where it was traded in for African people; the slave ships then continued to the Caribbean (mainly Santo Domingo) where the Africans were sold as slaves, many to work on sugar plantations. Ships returned to Bordeaux stuffed full of colonial goodies. The entire voyage took 18 months.

★ Top Tips

o Families with kids: don't miss the free Ten Works booklets for children available at the ticketing desk challenging young sleuths to find 10 different objects in the museum.

o Rent an audioguide (€2.50) at the entrance; the commentary lasts 2½ hours.

o The museum hosts fascinating temporary exhibitions; the schedule's online.

o In 2019 an exciting section was added to the permanent collection, covering modern Bordeaux history from 1800 to 1939.

✕ Take a Break

For a quick coffee, fresh juice or turbo-powered smoothie after the museum, duck across the road into Banana Café (p66).

Enjoy late breakfasts and veg-packed lunches at coffee shop Café Piha (p65).

Top Experience 📷

Admire Elegant Place de la Bourse

⊙ MAP P54, F4

Appropriately called place Royale when it was designed for Louis XV in the mid-18th century, this is Bordeaux's most elegant square. It was designed to open up the medieval city to the neighbouring river and world by way of the Atlantic, and both city walls and buildings were razed to make way for its magnificent horseshoe-shaped sweep on the banks of the Garonne.

Architecture

In keeping with architect Ange-Jacques Gabriel's design, drawn up in 1730 but not complete until after his death in 1775 (his sons subsequently oversaw the ambitious construction project), elegant palaces frame the square. The same architect designed the celebrated Château de Versailles near Paris and his classical architectural symmetry could not be more perfect or beautiful.

Hôtels Particuliers

On one side of the square stood **Hôtel des Fermes du Roy** (1735–38) or Ferme Générale, built in the 18th century to house the king's tax collectors and customs officers. Inside, the vast Salle de Dédouanement (Customs Hall) – 40m long and 30m wide, with sweeping vaulted ceiling – has been perfectly restored. On the other side of the square was **Palais de la Bourse** – an exact mirror copy of Hôtel des Fermes du Roy – in which the city's stock exchange was housed.

Musée National des Douanes

Opium pipes, impounded ostrich eggs, antique measuring scales, uniforms and scale models are among the eclectic curiosities exhibited in the unusual **National Customs Museum** (📞 09 70 27 57 66; www.musee-douanes.fr; 1 place de la Bourse; adult/child €3/free; ⏰ 10am-6pm Tue-Sun, free 1st Sun of month), at home today in the building on place de la Bourse where the city's first customs officers were stationed in the 1730s. The museum tells the story of French customs from the 18th century to the present day, and is even staffed by official French customs officers. Customs-themed art works displayed include contemporary French artist Ben's *Rien à déclarer* (Nothing to Declare) and French Impressionist Claude Monet's 1882 painting of the customs house, *Cabane des douaniers, effet d'après-midi*.

★ Top Tips

o It is worth the €2 to rent an audioguide at the Musée National des Douanes; count 1½ hours to complete the DIY tour.

o Snap a selfie with Euphrosyne, Aglaea and Thalia – three of the nine daughters of Zeus representing mirth, elegance and youth or beauty respectfully – at the Fontaine des Trois Grâces (Fountain of the Three Graces; 1869) in the centre of the square.

o Palais de la Bourse and its harem of elegant palaces, clustered in the pool of water created by the Miroir d'Eau (p56) across the square, makes for the ultimate Bordeaux Instagram shot.

✗ Take a Break

Grab a gourmet hot dog to take away from Woof (p60) and picnic on place de la Bourse.

Top Experience

Get Immersed in Fine Art at Musée des Beaux Arts

Occidental art from the Renaissance to the mid-20th century is on view at Bordeaux's Museum of Fine Arts, which occupies two wings of the majestic, 1771-built Palais Rohan or Hôtel de Ville, either side of elegant city park Jardin de la Mairie. Highlights include 17th-century Flemish, Dutch and Italian paintings. Bordeaux's native painters are also particularly well represented.

◎ MAP P54, A7

☏ 05 56 10 20 56

www.musba-bordeaux.fr

20 cours d'Albret

adult/child €5/free

⊙ 11am-6pm Wed-Mon

South Wing

Find here the museum's oldest work, *Vièrge de Pitié* (Virgin of Pity; 1469) by Flemish painter Hans Clot.

North Wing

Star turns here are works by French painters Eugène Delacroix and Renoir. *Les Quais de Bordeaux* (1892) portrays Bordeaux quays at dusk in winter by Impressionist Alfred Smith (1854–1932), born in Bordeaux to a Welsh father and Bordelais mother. The 'Landscapes & Animal Painting' room wows visitors with a monumental painting of white horses, *La foulaison du blé en Camargue* (Treading Wheat in the Camargue; 1899). This was the last (un-finished) painting by Bordeaux's Rosa Bonheur, one of France's most celebrated female artists who famously wore trousers when she worked. A portrait of her in her studio in 1893 shows her doing just this. Subsequent rooms include modern Bordeaux artists: Symbolist Odilon Redon (1840–1916), dot-mad Fauvist Albert Marquet (1975–47) and Cubist André Lhote (1855–1962).

Rosa Bonheur

No Bordeaux artist caused so much outrage in the 19th century as female realist painter Rosa Bonheur (1822–99). In 1855 she completed her most famous work, *The Horse Fair,* now in New York's Metropolitan Museum of Art. In 1894 she became first female artist to become an Officer of the French Legion of Honour. A forthright lesbian, Rosa wore shirts and trousers, smoked, hunted and made no bones about her fervent dislike of men. She lived with her first partner, Nathalie Micas, in Paris for 40 years and, fol-lowing Nathalie's death, romanced American painter Anna Elizabeth Klumpke. The trio are buried together in Paris' Cimitière du Père Lachaise.

★ Top Tips

o The museum has two wings, the South Wing (15th to 18th century) and North Wing (19th and 20th century), each with its own entrance.

o The museum sits within the Jardin de la Mairie, an elegant city park with a fountain, statues, manicured flower-beds and ample benches to enjoy a mindful moment.

o Watch for tempo-rary exhibitions held in the museum's annexe, **Galerie des Beaux Arts** (☑ 05 56 96 51 60; place du Colo-nel Raynal; adult/child €7/free; ⏰ 11am-6pm Wed-Mon).

o Check the website for monthly art lec-tures, themed guided tours and other activities for both adults and children.

✖ Take a Break

Indulge in post-museum brunch at Contrast (p60).

Serous coffee and delicious home-made cakes beckon at Horace (p62).

Walking Tour 🚶

Shop Bordelais-Style

*Provincial Bordeaux gives Paris a good run for
its money when it comes to on-trend boutique
shopping. The Bordelais share an enormous pride
in their city and its talented artisans, with a feast
of independent and historic shops and strips in
Saint-Pierre and Saint-Paul to prove it.*

Walk Facts

Start Cathédrale St-André
End Rue Ste-Catherine
Length 1.8km; one hour

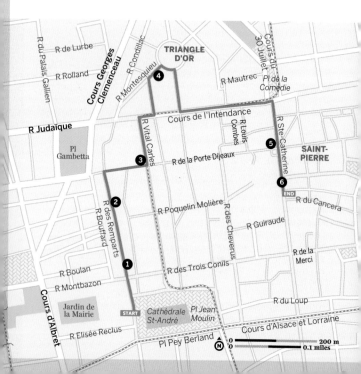

❶ Sisterly Fashion

Get acquainted with local fashion designers **Les Sisterettes** (☎09 81 95 63 23; www.lessisterette.fr; 60 rue des Remparts; ⏱noon-7pm Mon, 10am-7pm Tue-Sat), a stylish boutique for women by 'sisterettes' Céline and Amandine. Look for accessories by Bordelaise designer Camille and handmade jewellery by La Boutique d'Élodie.

❷ Made in Bordeaux

Homegrown design is god in Bordeaux. Discover the work of local trailblazers at **Baaam** (☎05 35 54 56 46; www.baaam.fr; rue des Remparts; ⏱10.30am-2pm & 3-7pm Mon-Sat), a beautifully arranged concept store specialising in homewares and hip lifestyle items made in the city or, at a push, elsewhere in France.

❸ France's Largest Independent Bookshop

Family-run bookshop **Mollat** (www.mollat.com; 15 rue Vital Carles; ⏱9.30am-7.30pm Mon-Sat), founded by Albert Mollat in 1896, packs five adjoining mansions with a labyrinth of books, ordered to sweet perfection on a mind-boggling 18km of bookshelves. French philosopher, writer and scholar Charles Montesquieu (1689–1755) aptly lived in one of the townhouses.

❹ Tomme de Bordeaux

Many a cheese-and-wine match made in heaven has been conceived at highly respected, boutique *fromagerie* **Jean d'Alos** (☎05 56 44 29 66.; www.jeandalos-fromager. com; 4 rue Montesquieu; ⏱9am-1pm & 3-7pm Tue-Thu, 9am-7pm Fri & Sat). Buy a chunk of Tomme de Bordeaux, a raw goat-milk cheese washed for several weeks in white Muscadet wine and encrusted in a peppery cocktail of herbs and spices.

❺ Galeries Lafayette

Outside, on the corner of rue Louis Combes and rue de la Porte Dijeaux, admire B&W prints of Bordeaux's iconic department store (p71) in the 1930s. Locals have shopped here since the 1900s when Les Dames de France – hence the 'DF' lettering on the shop's elegant neobaroque façade – opened; Paris' Galeries Lafayette bought it in 1985. The exquisite Naudet & Cie barometer encrusted on the building still functions.

❻ Rue Ste-Catherine

Paris has the Champs-Élysée, Marseille La Canebière, and Bordeaux, Europe's longest pedestrianised shopping strip called **rue Ste-Catherine**. The 1.25km street links place de la Comédie (north) with place de la Victoire (south). The Romans built it; urban planners kicked cars off it in the mid-1970s; and celebrity French architect Jean-Michel Wilmotte gave it a shiny new contemporary polish in 2000–2003.

Walking Tour

Renaissance Bordeaux

A stroll through Renaissance Bordeaux is a waltz through the oldest part of the city – an enchanting rabbit warren of narrow lanes, some cobbled, and hidden car-free squares in Saint-Paul built between the 14th and 16th centuries. Very much a golden period for the city, the wine flowed and beautiful palaces sprang up.

Walk Facts

Start place Fernand-Lafargue

End place Camille Jullian

Length 2.5km; two hours

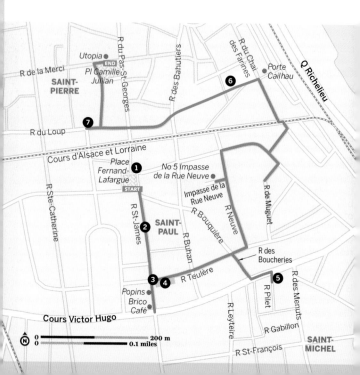

❶ Place Fernand-Lafargue

Start with *un café* at vintage L'Apollo (p65) on cafe-ringed place Fernand-Lafargue, abuzz with *la vie Bordelaise* (Bordeaux life). In the Middle Ages, this was the central market square.

❷ Rue St-James

Meander south along rue St-James, pausing to admire the detailed sculpted door at No 16 and windows at No 18. The street lies on the Way of St-James to Santiago de Compostela, hence its name. Look for the copper shell, symbol of the medieval pilgrimage route, encrusted in the street.

❸ City Gate

Walk beneath the 15th-century city gate and look back to admire its Grosse Cloche (p56). An icon of the city, the bell tower features on Bordeaux's coat of arms.

❹ Église St-Eloi

Outside the city gate, note the Gothic façade of Église St-Eloi, built in 1245 and the official church of the city mayor and his merry band of *jurats* who ran the city when Bordeaux was under English rule. Duck into trendy Popins (p70) to snap up a clip-on umbrella stand for your bike, unique to Bordeaux. Join locals queueing at Brico Café (p58) for a sugar-dusted *gâteau cheminée* to chomp while walking.

❺ Bordeaux's Oldest House

Walk east along rue Teulère. Turn right onto rue des Boucheries, left onto cours Victor Hugo, then right onto rue Pilet to view Bordeaux's oldest house in all its half-timbered glory at No 2. Backtrack to rue Teulère, continue a block east, and turn left onto rue Neuve where a dead-end alley squirrels away Bordeaux's other oldest house (5 impasse de la rue Neuve). The cobbles underfoot are the real McCoy 17th-century originals.

❻ Place du Palais

Continue north on rue Neuve and zig-zag onto extraordinarily narrow rue du Muguet, deemed the city's most picturesque street. Weave north to place du Palais, dominated in the Renaissance by **Palais de l'Olmbrière**, residence of the Dukes of Aquitaine and city parliament from 1462 to 1790. All that remains of the palace, demolished in 1800, is the city's only other remaining medieval city gate: Porte Cailhau (p56). Scale it for a 360-degree city panorama.

❼ Hôtel Ragueneau

Final port of call: Hôtel Ragueneau (1656), four blocks west at 71 rue du Loup. The former city archives are famed for the magnificent wisteria that, since 1860, showers the mansion's Renaissance-sculpted façade in a springtime riot of tiny purple flowers. End with lunch in a former Renaissance church at Utopia (p65).

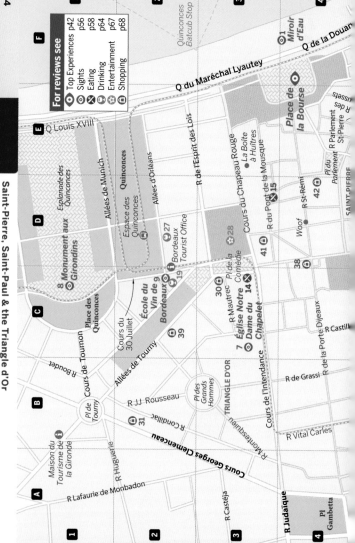

For reviews see

- ◉ Top Experiences p42
- ◉ Sights p56
- ✕ Eating p58
- 🍷 Drinking p64
- ✪ Entertainment p67
- 🛍 Shopping p68

Quinconces
Batcub Stop

◉ 1 Miroir d'Eau

Q de la Douan

Q de la Douan

Place de la Bourse

R des Russets

R Parlement St-Pierre

Pl du Parlement

SAINT-PIERRE

R St-Rémi

Q du Maréchal Lyautey

R de l'Esprit des Lois

Cours du Chapeau Rouge

La Boîte à Huîtres

R du Pont de la Mousque

✕ 15

Q Louis XVIII

Esplanade des Quinconces

Allées de Munich

Quinconces

Allées d'Orléans

Espace des Quinconces

◉ 8 Monument aux Girondins

Place des Quinconces

Cours de Tournon

R Boudet

Cours du 30 Juillet

École du Vin de Bordeaux

Allées de Tourny

◉ 27

🛈 Bordeaux Tourist Office

19

39

Pl de Tourny

🛈 Maison du Tourisme de la Gironde

R Huguerie

R JJ Rousseau

31

R Condillac

Pl des Grands Hommes

TRIANGLE D'OR

Cours Georges Clemenceau

R Montesquieu

R Mautrec

Pl de la Comédie

30

✕ 14

◉ 7 Église Notre Dame du Chapelet

28

41

38

Woof

42

SAINT-PIERRE

Cours de l'Intendance

R de Grassi

R Vital Carles

R de la Porte Dijeaux

R Castill

R de la Porte Dijeaux

R Lafaurie de Monbadon

R Castéja

R Judaïque

Pl Gambetta

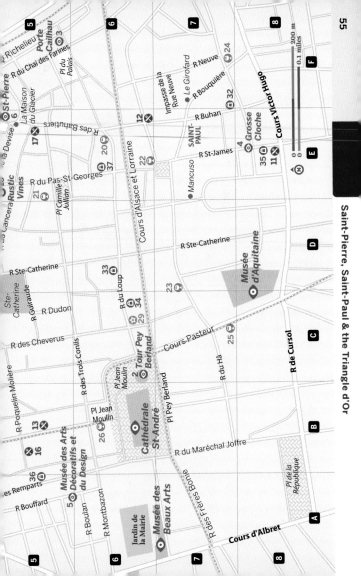

Saint-Pierre, Saint-Paul & the Triangle d'Or

Sights

Miroir d'Eau
FOUNTAIN

1 MAP P54, F4

A fountain of sorts, the Miroir d'Eau is the world's largest reflecting pool. Covering an area of 3450 sq metres of black granite on the quayside opposite the imposing Palais de la Bourse, the 'water mirror' provides hours of entertainment on warm sunny days when the reflections in its thin slick of water – drained and refilled every half-hour – are stunning. Every 23 minutes a dense fog-like vapour is ejected for three minutes to add to the fun (and photo opportunities). (Water Mirror; place de la Bourse; admission free; ⏰10am-10pm summer)

Tour Pey Berland
TOWER

2 MAP P54, C6

This gargoyled, 50m-high Flamboyant Gothic belfry was built for the adjoining cathedral between 1440 and 1466. Its spire was added

Cent Saver

Consider investing in the Bordeaux **Métropole City Pass** (www.bordeauxcitypass.com; €29/39/46 for 24/48/72 hours), covering admission to 20 museums and monuments. It also includes a free guided tour and unlimited use of public buses, trams and boats.

in the 19th century, and in 1863 it was topped off with the shiny gold statue of Notre Dame de l'Aquitaine (Our Lady of Aquitaine). Scaling the tower's 231 narrow steps rewards you with a spectacular city panorama. Only 19 visitors are allowed up at any one time, so be prepared to queue in season. (📞05 56 81 26 25; www.pey-berland.fr; place Pey-Berland; adult/child €6/free; ⏰10am-1.15pm & 2-6pm Tue-Sun Jun-Sep, 10am-12.30pm & 2-5.30pm Tue-Sun Oct-May)

Porte Cailhau
MONUMENT

3 MAP P54, F5

The main entrance into medieval Bordeaux, this grandiose 15th-century city gate was built to celebrate King Charles VII's victory at the Battle of Fornovo (1495) and conquest of the kingdom of Naples. The campaign in Italy gave the French a taste for the Renaissance and the 35m-high city gate could well be a Renaissance chateau in miniature form with its elegant slate roof, witch-hat turrets and castle-like windows peering out across the river above the Gothic archway. (📞05 56 48 04 24; place du Palais; adult/child €5/free; ⏰10am-1pm & 2-6pm)

Grosse Cloche
BELFRY

4 MAP P54, E8

Guarded by a twinset of witch-hat capped towers, this Gothic belfry was built on the vestiges of 13th-century protective ramparts and later served as both a prison and the bell tower of the nearby Hôtel de Ville (city hall). The huge bell, born as Armande-Louise in 1775 (bells always have names), weighs a hefty 7750kg and required 14 pairs of oxen to hoist it into place. (1 rue St-James; admission €5; ⏱guided tours 2-5pm Sat Mar-Nov)

Musée des Arts Décoratifs et du Design
GALLERY

5 ◉ MAP P54, A5

Faience pottery, porcelain, gold, iron, glasswork and furniture are displayed at the small Decorative Arts and Design Museum, at home in an elegant golden-stone *hôtel particulier* (private mansion) dating to 1779. Temporary exhibitions cost extra. Its cafe, with alfresco courtyard seating, is a peaceful spot to linger. (☎05 56 10 14 00; www.madd-bordeaux.fr; 39 rue Bouffard; adult/child €5/3, free 1st Sun of month; ⏱11am-6pm Wed-Mon)

Église St-Pierre
CHURCH

6 ◉ MAP P54, E5

Saint-Pierre's enchanting labyrinth of narrow lanes inevitably leads to the predominantly 15th-century church around which the medieval neighbourhood flourished. From 1152, when Aquitaine fell under the English crown, it served as the parish church for many English nobles and merchants later buried here. Inside the church, admire spectacular 19th-century stained-glass windows (those in the left aisle illustrate the story of St-Peter), the baroque altarpiece

Porte Cailhau

and a supremely beautiful wooden 17th-century Pietà sculpted in wood. (place St-Pierre; admission free; ☺hours vary)

Église Notre Dame du Chapelet
CHURCH

7 ◉ MAP P54, C3

On 17 April 1828 the funeral of Romantic Spanish painter Francisco Goya (1746–1828) took place in this magnificent French Baroque church, a stone's throw from where the artist spent the last years of his life at 59 cours de l'Intendance. The church, with striking sculpted façade and light-flooded interior, formed part of a new monastery built for Dominican monks between 1684 and 1707. Its acoustics are exceptional and catching a free organ concert is well worth it. (place du Chapelet; ☺2-9pm Mon, 7am-9pm Tue-Sat, 10am-9pm Sun)

Monument aux Girondins
MONUMENT

8 ◉ MAP P54, C1

This imposing fountain on vast square and public-transport hub Esplanade des Quinconces is a riot of horses. It was created between 1894 and 1902 in honour of the Girondins, a group of moderate, bourgeois National Assembly deputies during the French Revolution, 22 of whom were executed in 1793 after being convicted of counter-revolutionary activities. (Esplanade des Quinconces)

École du Vin de Bordeaux
WINE

9 ◉ MAP P54, C2

Serious students of the grape can enrol at this highly regarded wine school inside the Maison du Vin de Bordeaux (Bordeaux House of Wine). It hosts introductory two-hour workshops the last Saturday of each month and daily from July to September (€32), plus more complex two- to three-day courses from May to October. (Bordeaux Wine School; ☎05 56 00 22 85; www.bordeaux.com; 3 cours du 30 juillet; introductory workshops €32)

Rustic Vines
CYCLING

10 ◉ MAP P54, E5

Private and small-group (2 to 8 people) tours year-round, by minivan, bicycle and e-bike in and around Bordeaux. Count €149 for a full-day group tour by minivan with lunch and wine-tastings, and €135 for a full-day guided e-bike ride to and around St-Émilion. (☎09 86 41 88 83; http://rusticvines tours.com; 26 rue de la Devise)

Eating

Brico Café
HUNGARIAN €

11 ◈ MAP P54, E8

The smell of freshly baked bread is irresistible at this hole-in-the-wall bakery, run by Hungarian baker Andras Csuha near the Grosse Cloche belfry. His savoury *borek* (pastries) stuffed with various

Medieval to Modern Bordeaux

In 1152, as part of Eleanor of Aquitaine's dowry in her marriage to the would-be King Henry II of England, Bordeaux fell under English rule. Thus began a golden period for the city. The English fondness for the region's red wine provided the impetus for Bordeaux's enduring international reputation for quality wines. King Henry II gained favour with locals by granting them tax-free trade status with England and Bordeaux soon enjoyed a buoyant wine trade with *les anglais*. From 1227 new walls were built, incorporating the artisan quartier of Saint-Paul – home to iron forgeries, carpenters and blacksmiths.

Increasing hostility between the English and French degenerated into the Hundreds Year War in 1337, fought on and off until Charles VII's decisive victory at the Battle of Castillon (1453), ending the war and annexing the Duchy of Aquitaine – and Bordeaux – back to France. To prove his absolute authority, Charles VII had huge fortress Château Trompette built on Esplanades des Quinconces (razed in 1818 to make way for today's square) and Château du Hâ (one tower remains) constructed on the city's southern fringe. In 1495, to honour Charles VII's conquest of the Kingdom of Naples, the Porte Cailhau city gate was constructed by the river. Renaissance ideas of scientific and geographic scholarship and discovery assumed a new importance; Bordeaux University (1441) became a hotbed of intellectual activity.

The city parliament, in existence since 1462, served as a voice-piece for Humanists in its ranks and it's thanks to the level-headedness of moderate humanist, writer and philosopher Michel de Montaigne (1533–93) – Bordeaux mayor from 1581 to 1585 – that the city survived the Reformation and Wars of Religion between the Huguenots (French protestants), Catholic League and Monarchy relatively unscathed.

Eighteenth-century urban planners razed city walls and dark, narrow streets to transform the medieval city into modern Bordeaux. Place de la Bourse was landscaped; a bridge was built in 1775 to link the left and right banks; riverside quays were constructed; and the cupola-crowned Grand Théâtre (1780) – a model for architect Charles Garnier's opera house in Paris – opened. The arrival of the railway in 1837 only bolstered port activity still further.

fillings are lunch-perfect, but it is the *gâteau cheminée* ('chimney cake'; a hollow, cylindrical-shaped brioche covered in sugar, cinnamon, almonds or grilled hazelnuts) that steals the show.

Gourmet Fast Food

Trust the Bordelais to come up with fast food that is local, delicious and designed solely to appease culinary cravings of busy gourmets. Should local, freshly shucked Arcachon oysters be your vice, make a beeline for **La Boîte à Huîtres** (Map p54, E3; ☑ 05 56 81 64 97; 36 cours du Chapeau Rouge; 12 oysters €16-32; ☺ noon-2pm & 6-11pm Tue-Sat, 10am-2pm Sun) aka The Oyster Box. Traditionally they're served with sausage but you can have them in a number of different forms, including with that other southwest delicacy, foie gras. Ask for them to be packed up so you can take them away for a riverfront picnic.

For a swift street-food bite between sights, duck into **Woof** (Map p54, D4; www.wearewoof.com; 61 rue St-Rémi; hot dogs €3.50-7; ☺ noon-10.30pm Tue-Sat, 6-10.30pm Sun) for a gourmet hot dog – to eat in, in the attractive Scandinavian-styled interior, or to take out. Bread is organic and tasty homemade fillings to accompany your *chien chaud* include caramelised onions, cream cheese, guacamole and sun-dried tomatoes.

(☑ 06 47 44 85 94; 115 cours Victor Hugo; €3.50-6; ☺ 10am-1pm & 3-10pm Wed-Sun)

Kitchen Garden   VEGETARIAN €

12 🍴 MAP P54, E6

A fresh, seasonal cuisine bursting with veggies is what the Kitchen Garden predictably cooks up. Water jugs come stuffed with mint and lemon, and there's a definite floral 'n' vegetal theme going on in the motley collection of prints strung on the bright-white brick wall. Lunch on homemade soup and an imaginatively topped *tartine* (open sandwich). Fantastic juices and smoothies too. (☑ 09 83 37 76 10; www.kitchengarden.fr; 22 rue Ste-Colombe; mains €10-15;

☺ 9.30am-8pm Mon-Wed, 9.30am-10pm Thu-Sat, 10.30am-3pm Sun)

Contrast   BREAKFAST €

13 🍴 MAP P54, B5

'In Brunch We Trust' is the strap-line of this brilliant address serving indulgent breakfast and brunch all day. Be it homemade granola, pan-cakes, lavish fruit salads, eggs or toast topped with avocado or scarlet beetroot humous, well-travelled creative duo Laura and Mamadou deliver. Stylish cane furniture, soft gold-stone walls, white walls and vases of fresh flowers create a sunny, mellow ambiance. (☑ 05 57 99 45 03; www.facebook.com/contrast brunch; 40 rue Vital Carles; brunch €25; ☺ 9.30am-6.30pm Mon, Wed & Fri, 10.30am-6.30pm Sat & Sun)

Le Bordeaux

CAFE €€

14  MAP P54, C3

To dine à la Gordon Ramsay without breaking the bank, reserve a table at his elegant belle époque brasserie with an interesting Anglo-French hybrid cuisine – local Arcachon oysters, fish 'n' chips, Gascon pork pie with piccalilli, braised beef chuck, hand-cut tartare – and a parasol-shaded pavement terrace overlooking busy place de la Comédie. Weekend brunch (€68) is a local hot date. (☎05 57 30 43 46; https://bordeaux.intercontinental.com; 2-5 place de la Comédie; 2-/3-course lunch menu from €29/39, mains €27; ⏰7am-10.30pm)

Le Bouchon Bordelais

FRENCH €€

15 MAP P54, D3

Seasonal market produce and a generous pinch of creativity form the backbone of this *bistrot coloré* (colourful bistro), tucked down a backstreet lane between place de la Bourse and place de la Comédie. With its exposed stone walls and terracotta floor tiles, Le Bouchon Bordelais' interior decor is 100% traditional and quaint – the menu is not. (☎05 56 44 33 00; www.bouchon-bordelais.com; 2 rue Courbin; lunch mains €10-16, 2/3/7-course dinner menu from €28/39/55)

Oysters

Saint-Pierre, Saint-Paul & the Triangle d'Or Eating

Ice Break

Break old-town meanderings in medieval Saint-Pierre with an ice cream from local institution **La Maison du Glacier** (Map p54, E5; ☑ 05 40 54 65 96; www.facebook.com/lamaison duglacier; 1 place St-Pierre; 1/2/3 scoops €2.70/4.30/5.80; ⏱ 1.30-6.30pm). There are 80-odd unusual flavours – all organic – to choose from, including green tea, almond, ginger, apple, quince, chestnut and rhubarb. Summertime seating spills across pretty place St-Pierre.

Horace   INTERNATIONAL €€

16 🍽 MAP P54, B5

Whatever the time of day, Horace can do no wrong. Outstanding speciality coffee roasts (including Oven Heaven beans roasted locally), sophisticated fruit- and veg-packed breakfasts, home-made brioches and breads, and lunch/dinner menus bursting with creativity are the quality hallmarks of this coffee shop, owned by the same talented barista as Bordeaux's Black List (p43). Sunday brunch (€21) is a sell-out every week.

Horace's chai latte is particularly superb. For non-coffee lovers, the aromatic rose or orange-flower flavoured warm milks, carefully curated *grands crus* of artisan hot chocolates and Bordeaux-brewed craft beers by Brasserie Azimut are all equally heavenly. (☑ 05 56 90 01 93; 40 rue Poquelin Molière; mains €8-14; ⏱ 8.30am-6.30pm Mon, to 9.30pm Tue-Fri, 9.30am-9.30pm Sat, 9.30am-6.30pm Sun)

Le Davoli   MODERN FRENCH €€

17 🍽 MAP P54, E5

When the urge for more refined dining strikes, reserve a table at this gourmet station in Saint-Pierre with talented chef David Grangier in the kitchen. Contemporary art adorns the medieval gold-stone walls and tasting menus feature clams, wild prawns, veal, sole, asparagus and other refined seasonal products. End with the sensational lemon dessert – lemon in several guises. (☑ 05 56 48 22 19; www.ledavoli.com; 13 rue des Bahutiers; 2-course lunch menu €24-28, 3-/4-/5-course dinner menus €42/56/64; ⏱ 12.15-1.20pm & 7.30-9.30pm Tue-Sat)

Le Petit Commerce   SEAFOOD €€

18 🍽 MAP P54, E5

This iconic bistro, with dining rooms both sides of a narrow pedestrian street and former Michelin-starred chef Stéphane Carrade in the kitchen, is the star turn of the trendy Saint-Pierre quarter. It's best known for its excellent seafood menu that embraces everything from Arcachon sole and oysters to eels, lobsters and *chipirons* (baby squid) fresh from St-Jean de Luz.

End your meal, as locals do, with a bowl of *riz au lait à l'orange* (orange-perfumed rice pudding). Check its Facebook page to see what's cooking on the day's excellent-value lunchtime menu. (☎ 05 56 79 76 58; 22 rue Parlement St-Pierre; 2-course lunch menu €16, mains €15-26; ⏱ 10am-1am)

Le Pressoir d'Argent
GASTRONOMY €€€

Dining at the Michelin two-starred, gastronomic restaurant of 18th-century Grand Hôtel de Bordeaux (see 14 ✕ Map p54, C3) is staggering. Presided over by celebrity British chef Gordon Ramsay, the kitchen uses the finest regional produce to create the ultimate sophisticated cuisine. Order lobster to see the

City Panoramas

Saint-Pierre's elegant 19th-century **Pont de Pierre** (1819–22) is the oldest bridge across the Garonne in Bordeaux and aptly proffers some of the finest city-scape views; factor ample bridge lingering into your itinerary. For bird's-eye views of the city – and to get your bearings before delving in – hike up Porte Cailhau (p56) or the cathedral's impressive bell tower (p56).

restaurant's rare, solid-silver Christofle lobster press – just one of five in the world – in action. (The Silver Press; ☎ 05 57 30 43 42;

Pont de Pierre

www.ghbordeaux.com; 2-5 place de la Comédie; 6-course tasting menu €185, mains €87-110; ⏱7-9pm Tue-Sat)

Drinking

Night Beach BAR

There is no finer, more elegant or romantic rooftop bar in Bordeaux than this achingly hip drinking-and-hobnobbing joint on the 7th floor of historic Grand Hôtel de Bordeaux (see 14 ✕ Map p54, C3). Views of the city, River Garonne and the vineyards beyond are a panoramic 360 degrees.

French-chic seating is sofa-style beneath parasols, and DJ sets play at weekends. Opening times are weather-dependent. (https://bordeaux.intercontinental.com; 2-5

place de la Comédie, 7th fl, Grand Hôtel de Bordeaux; ⏱7pm-1am late May-late Sep)

Bar à Vin WINE BAR

19 🚌 MAP P54, C2

The decor – herringbone parquet, grandiose stained glass depicting the godly Bacchus, and sky-high ceiling – matches the reverent air that fills this wine bar inside the hallowed halls of the Maison du Vin de Bordeaux. Dozens of Bordeaux wines are served by the glass (€3.50–8) which, paired with a cheese or charcuterie platter, transport foodies straight to heaven. Gracious sommeliers know their *vin*.

At home in the historic Maison Gobineau (1789), the bar's elegant

Place Camille Jullian (p66)

interior dates to 1951. (📞 05 56 00 43 47; http://baravin.bordeaux.com; 8 cours du 30 Juillet; 🕑 11am-10pm Mon-Sat)

CanCan
COCKTAIL BAR

🔟 MAP P54, E6

'Coquetels et flonflon' (meaning 'cocktails and music') is the strapline of this achingly cool speakeasy by Parisian duo Romain and Clément. The vibe is fashionably retro, the decor hardcore vintage, and the sound a fun mix of New Orleans jazz, 1990s hip hop and soul. DJs play strictly vinyl every Thursday from 9pm, and Sunday is jazz night. (📞 05 56 06 55 11; www.cancanbordeaux.com; 7 rue du Cerf Volant; 🕑 8pm-1am Wed-Sun)

Utopia
CAFE, BAR

21 MAP P54, E5

At home in an old church, this much-venerated art address is a local institution – its sunny terrace alone is fabulous. Art-house cinema, mellow cafe, hot lunch spot and bar rolled into one, it is one of the top addresses in the city to mingle with locals over a drink, tartine (open sandwich), salad, soup or smoothie any time of day. (📞 05 56 79 39 25; www.cafe-utopia.fr; 3 place Camille Jullian; 🕑 10am-1am summer, to 10.30pm winter)

L'Apollo
BAR

22 MAP P54, E6

No place buzzes with a local Bordelais crowd quite like the Apollo, a

Roasted in Bordeaux

World cultures unite at Café Piha, a tropical-styled coffee shop named after the bay in New Zealand where French barista Pierre Guerin learnt about kite-surfing – and coffee. Paper-brown sachets of his medium-roasted espresso beans or lighter filter roasts, all roasted in situ with much local savvy and Bordelaise *amour,* are a perfect souvenir to take home.

fabulous neighbourhood bar with burnt-orange, paint-peeling façade and busy pavement terrace. In the best of pub fashion, it has a pool table and a fantastic line-up of DJ sets, music parties and 'apéro mix' soirées belting out funk, soul and reggae. (📞 05 56 01 25 05; www.apollobar.fr; 19 place Fernand Lafargue; 🕑 11.30am-1.30am Mon-Sat; 📶)

Café Piha
COFFEE

23 MAP P54, D7

The door handle alone – part of a coffee machine – says it all: this new-generation coffee shop is cool. Lounge on cushioned bench seating in a faintly exotic, Amazon-styled interior and take your pick of speciality coffee and brewing method (espresso, Chemex, V60 etc). Beans are roasted in the roastery out back and you can buy sachets to go. Granola-fuelled

La Vie Bordelaise

Lounging on a summertime cafe or restaurant terrace is a supremely fine essential of *la vie bordelaise* (Bordelais life). Pedestrian place St-Pierre and place du Parlement, both in the heart of Saint-Pierre, are ringed with delightful cafe terraces and buzz with drinkers any time of day. Place Camille Jullian – place Ca-Ju to locals – is another enchanting square to linger over a drink. Alfresco terraces on stone-paved rue des Faussets (off place St-Pierre) and rue de la Devise are likewise idyllic on warm summer evenings.

breakfasts (€3–7.50) are served until noon and lunch (noon–3pm) might be a filet mignon marinated in honey mustard or avocado toast.

Reservations are essential for weekend brunch (€20). Laptops welcome. (📞09 67 80 83 42; www. cafepiha.com; 69 rue des Ayres; ⏰9am-4.30pm Mon & Wed-Fri, 10am-5pm Sat, 10am-4pm Sun; 🛜)

Au Nouveau Monde   CRAFT BEER

24 🚇 MAP P54, F7

Why does it come as no surprise to learn that France's first officially certified organic pub is in Bordeaux? Run with passion and panache by Quebecois Etienne, the brew bar has a tasty gastropub on the ground floor and artisan microbrewery in the basement. Everything – from its six house beers to the homemade burgers and inspired beer-cooked risotto – is 100% organic. (📞09 81 18 00 54; www.facebook.com/AuNouveauMonde.Bordeaux; 2 rue des Boucheries; ⏰noon-2am Thu-Sat, 11am-2am Sun, 6pm-midnight Mon, noon-1am Tue & Wed)

Banana Café   COFFEE

25 🚇 MAP P54, C7

What with its fabulous gluten-free cooking, chic interior design and Soundcloud page featuring the fantastic playlists spun here during Sunday brunch, Banana Café is one cool chick. Well-travelled British-French duo Kelly and Thibault are the creative talent behind the coffee shop, across the street from the Musée d'Aquitaine.

On weekend evenings, baby-pink candles add a romantic glow to the chapel-like back room. Arrive 11.30am on the dot to snag a table for weekend brunch. (📞05 56 23 33 39; http://bananacafe bordeaux.com; 5 cours Pasteur; ⏰10am-6pm Tue-Thu, 10am-6pm & 7.30-10.30pm Fri & Sat, 10am-5pm Sun)

Les Mots Bleues CAFE

6 MAP P54, B6

Books to tempt and be browsed casually sit on shelves in the contemporary blue-and-white interior of this peaceful coffee shop near the cathedral. It's filled each morning with the comforting aroma of baking from the tiny kitchen. The homemade cakes, cookies, crumbles and other sweet treats are all delicious, as are the unusual organic sparkling fruit juices (apricot and thyme, kiwi and saffron, blackcurrant and mint) made by Bordeaux's Unaju.

It has lunchtime salads to take away too. (www.facebook.com/lesmotsbleusofficiel; 3 rue place Jean Moulin; ⊙9am-6pm Tue-Sat)

Le Monseigneur CLUB

27 MAP P54, D2

Don your dancing shoes and hit the oldest nightclub in town (and about the only one in the centre) for some serious 1970s, '80s and '90s pop.

Admission includes one non-alcoholic drink. (☑05 56 44 89 60; http://lemonseigneur.com; 42 allée d'Orléans; admission €13; ⊙11.30pm-7am Wed-Sat)

Entertainment

Grand Théâtre THEATRE, OPERA

28 ⭐ MAP P54, D3

Designed by Victor Louis (of Chartres Cathedral fame), this grand 18th-century theatre stages operas, ballets and concerts of

place du Parlement

orchestral and chamber music.
(☎ 05 56 00 85 95; www.opera-bor
deaux.com; place de la Comédie)

Le Fiacre
LIVE MUSIC

29 ⭐ MAP P54, C6

A longstanding veteran of 20-odd
years on the drinking and music
scene, Le Fiacre continues to pull
in the crowds with its live rock
concerts and fantastic DJ sets.

Expect live gigs most weeks
on Thursday to Saturday from
8pm. Otherwise, beer is the
drink to order at this gutsy *bar
à bières*. (☎ 06 20 11 07 30; www.
facebook.com/pg/fiacrebordeaux; 42
rue Cheverus; ⏲ 6am-2am Mon-Fri,
7.30am-2am Sat)

Shopping

L'Intendant
WINE

30 🔒 MAP P54, C3

Welcome to what must be the
grandest wine shop in the whole
of France. A magnificent central
staircase spiralling up five floors is
surrounded by cylindrical shelves
holding 15,000 bottles of regional
wine at this highly respected *cav-
iste* (wine cellar).

Bottle prices range from €7
to thousands of euros. Watch for
tastings most Saturdays. (www.
intendant.com; 2 allées de Tourny;
⏲ 10am-7.30pm Mon-Sat)

L'Intendant

Chocolaterie Saunion

CHOCOLATE

§1 🔒 MAP P54, B2

Follow local gourmets to this exquisite, oh-so-bourgeois chocolate shop, run by the same family since 1893. Fourth-generation chocolate-maker Thierry Lalet is at the helm today, crafting gold-foil-wrapped Galliens de Bordeaux almond nougat, praline and hazelnut chocolate bonbon), Guinettes kirsch-soaked cherries enrobed in dark chocolate) and chewy Niniches Bordelaises (honey, milk and chocolate caramels) to die for. (📞05 56 48 05 75; www.saunion. fr; 56 cours Georges Clemenceau; ⏱2-7.15pm Mon, 9.30am-12.30pm & 2.30-7.15pm Tue-Sat)

Serendipity

HOMEWARES

§2 🔒 MAP P54, F7

Romantic and youthful, this delightful *cabinet de convivialité* inspires bags of instant feel-good factor. After several years in Paris, Claire Chabellard returned to her native Bordeaux to create this colourful Ali Baba's cave of beautiful, thoughtful objects for the home. Think 'Follow your Dreams' notebooks, Sass & Belle gifts and accessories, personalised jewellery, hanging flower pots and all sorts.

Serendipity also runs craft workshops (origami, candle-making, sewing, flower arranging etc); check its Facebook page. 📞07 69 60 02 22; www.facebook.

Street Entertainment

With its landmark historic clocks and street musicians hammering out entertaining beats, **place de la Comédie** is a favourite meeting place for locals and street buskers. Breakdancers and skateboarders congregate beneath the arches of the Grand Théâtre.

com/serendipitybdx; 26 rue Buhan; ⏱11am-7pm Tue-Thu, 11am-7.30pm Fri & Sat)

Blue Madone

VINTAGE

33 🔒 MAP P54, D6

Vintage designer fashion for men and women is the mainstay of Mathilde Milande's exquisitely arranged boutique, peppered from head to toe with an enchanting medley of retro lampshades, furniture and plants. Part of the space ensnares the in situ *ateliers* (workshops) of seven local designers specialising in jewellery, floral art, painted textiles, leatherwork, fashion and upholstery. Watch them at work. (📞05 57 30 25 13; https://blue madone.com; 59 rue du Loup; ⏱11am-7pm Tue-Sat)

Freep'Show Vintage

VINTAGE

34 🔒 MAP P54, C6

Old vinyls plaster the walls, retro dial-up telephones provide a

Vinyls for Lunch

Shopping and food are inevitably intertwined in foodie Bordeaux: browse collectible vinyls over a craft beer and sassy plate of whisky-infused pulled pork or mint- and coconut-laced tuna ceviche at **Mancuso** (Map p54, E7; 📞09 87 12 38 15; www.cafemancuso. com; 24 rue Ravez; ⏰10am-8pm Tue & Wed, to 11pm Thu & Fri, 11am-11pm Sat, record boutique 1-7pm Tue-Thu, 11am-8pm Fri & Sat), France's first audio-cantine. It is named after New York DJ David Mancuso, who made the Loft private parties so famous in NYC during the 1970s. Dedicated audiophiles can play and listen to vinyls – all sounds – over coffee or cocktails, a simple ceviche or salad lunch (€7–14), or shared evening plates (€3–16).

decorative touch and the opening hours are scrawled on a vintage TV set at this Pandora's box of a boutique selling vintage fashion – casual in the main – for men and women. Allow ample browsing time – the vintage hi-fi gear is really quite mesmerising. (📞07 82 59 36 84; www.freepshow.com; 80 rue du Loup; ⏰11am-7pm Mon-Sat)

Popins
SPORTS & OUTDOORS

35 🅐 MAP P54, E8

Only in Bordeaux, a city known for its rampant bicycle culture, could a shop come up with such an inspired invention: clip-on umbrella stands for bikes, allowing urban-cool Bordelais to pedal around town in the rain in comfort. This trendy bike shop also sells floral seat cushions, bags, helmets and most other imaginable bike accessories in dozens of different patterns and designs. (📞09 52

93 42 25; http://popins.fr; 55 rue St-James; ⏰10am-7pm Mon-Sat)

Chez Delphine
FOOD

36 🅐 MAP P54, A5

An old-fashioned cherry-red bicycle with worn leather seat and wicker basket, casually propped up outside, beckons gourmets and romantics into this gorgeous cheese shop on pedestrian rue des Ramparts. The tantalising pong of hundreds of different cheeses, many local or regional and dozens ripened in situ by female *fromagère* and *affineuse* extraordinaire Delphine Lapena, is heaven for cheese aficionados.

Specialities include a creamy camembert studded with figs and hazelnuts, and nutty mature gouda fashioned like sticks of nougat. Pair over lunch (menu €19) with a full-bodied Bordeaux red for a match made in heaven. (📞05

56 48 06 19; 44 rue des Remparts;
⊙10.30am-1pm & 3.30-7pm Tue-Sat)

Fromagerie Deruelle FOOD

37 🔒 MAP P54, E6

Originally from Lyon, Elodie Deruelle is the female prowess behind this exceptional cheese shop and *épicerie* (grocery). The choice of artisan dairy products, Lyonnaise *charcuterie* (cured meat), 150 cheese types and homemade delicacies is overwhelmingly tempting. Don't leave without purchasing a chunk of Elodie's famous cheesecake. (📞05 57 83 04 15; https://fromagerie-deruelle.com; 66 rue du Pas-Saint-Georges; ⊙4-7.30pm Mon, 10am-1.30pm & 4-7.30pm Tue-Sat)

Galeries Lafayette DEPARTMENT STORE

38 🔒 MAP P54, D4

Duck into the city's flagship department store, at home in an elegant Art Nouveau building from the 1900s, for a one-stop shop for women and children's fashion, accessories, homewares, books, luggage and stationary.

And yes, this is a younger sibling of Paris' mythical Galeries Lafayette, open in the capital since 1893.

For menswear pop across the road to **Galeries Lafayette – L'Homme** (12 2 rue de la Porte Dijeaux), in a stunningly renovated building from 1927 on rue Porte

Galeries Lafayette

Dijeaux. (📞05 56 90 92 71; www. galerieslafayette.com/magasin -bordeaux; 11-19 rue Sainte-Catherine; 🕙10am-8pm Mon-Sat, 11am-7pm Sun)

Chocolaterie Cadiot-Badie

CHOCOLATE

39 🔒 MAP P54, C2

Exquisite boxes of jellied fruits, chocolates and pralines tempt at this historic *chocolaterie* with an original interior of marble counters and gilded ceiling from 1826. For a sweet taste of Bordeaux, try a Diamant Noir (literally 'black diamond') – a dark chocolate-enrobed ganache truffle made from grape pulp macerated in Bordeaux wine. (📞05 56 44 24 22; https://cadiot-badie.com; 26 allées

de Tourny; 🕙10am-7pm Mon & Sat, 9.30am-7pm Tue-Fri)

Archibald & Zoé

FASHION & ACCESSORIES

40 🔒 MAP P54, E4

Shop for prêt à porter fashion for women and children, shoes, accessories and homewares – all 100% made in France – in this stylish concept store. Interesting finds include French-made 1083 jeans in organic cotton, gorgeous tote bags by Bordeaux's very own Cocorico, artisan candles that smell like fresh laundry or school paper glue, and organic beauty products by Happycuriennes. (📞09 83 00 60 89; www.facebook.com/ArchibaldEt Zoe; 26 rue Parlement Saint-Pierre;

Le Comptoir

(⏱10am-1.30pm & 2.15-7pm Tue-Fri, 10am-7pm Sat)

Le Comptoir
FOOD & DRINKS

41 🔒 MAP P54, D3

Rev up taste buds in this gourmet boutique selling local and regional food and drink specialities. Be tempted by local cheese, *canalés* (sandcastle-shaped cakes from Bordeaux), *bouchons de Bordeaux* (cork-shaped pastries filled with almonds), *raisins au Sauternes* (chocolate-enrobed raisins soaked in Sauternes wine), salted caramels, chocolate sardines, olive oils, sauces and condiments, craft beers, wine... The list is endless. (www.lecomptoirbordelais. com; 1 rue Piliers de Tutelle; ⏱9am-7.30pm)

w.a.n.
HOMEWARES

42 🔒 MAP P54, D4

'Slow design' is the driver behind this Pandora's Box of a boutique, packed to the rafters with innova-

The Golden Triangle

Bordeaux's famous **Triangle d'Or** (Golden Triangle) is framed by three grand boulevards: cours de l'Intendance (south) and cours Georges Clemenceau (west), both lined with upmarket shops and designer boutiques; and Allées de Tourny (east), home to historic chocolate shops.

tive design objects, homewares, clothing, knick-knacks and trinkets – all made in France or, as the shop motto explains, 'Made in *pas trop loin*' (not too far away). It's a lovely space to browse for gifts. Spiral downstairs to the cellar to uncover contemporary sculptures and art works by local artists. Opening hours are very exact. (Wagon à Nanomètre; 📞05 56 48 15 41; www.wanweb.fr; 1 rue des Lauriers; ⏱10.02am-7.04pm Mon-Sat)

Explore ◈

Saint-Michel & Capucins-Victoire

South of the historic centre, two landmark churches – Gothic Basilique St-Michel and Romanesque Église Ste-Croix – tether the vibrant neighbourhoods of Saint-Michel and Sainte-Criox, known for their antique shopping. A colourful pot-pourri of street markets provides a melting pot for a diverse ethnic population, while Bordeaux's sizeable student population gravitates to cafe terraces on place de la Victoire and around the city's premier food market, Marché des Capucins.

Get your bearings and a coffee on student-filled place de la Victoire (p82), then stroll east to market-square place des Capucins: the covered market (p89) is only open mornings so arrive early to ensure the pick of produce and oysters for lunch at Chez Jean-Mi (p83). Explore Basilique St-Michel (p76) on place Reynard (invariably buzzing with an open-air flea market) and unsung Romanesque Église Ste-Croix (p82) in the afternoon. Dine at La Tupina (p84) and, come dark, explore the riverside quays south of Sainte-Croix. Hit La Plage (p89), the city's largest mainstream nightclub.

Getting There & Around

🚊 **Tram** Line C northbound from Gare St-Jean or southbound from Esplanade des Quinconces to stops Porte de Bourgogne, St-Michel or Ste-Croix.

Neighbourhood Map on p80

Place de la Victoire (p82) TRABANTOS/SHUTTERSTOCK ©

Top Experience

Admire the Flamboyant Gothic Basilique St-Michel

Its blackened facade begs for a scrub and polish, but the imposing Flamboyant Gothic architecture of St-Michel's iconic basilica remains impressive. Construction work began in the 14th century and continued for more than 200 years. To feel the pulse of local life, join the throbbing gaggles of Bordelais hanging out on the two squares framing their truly magnificent 'village' church.

◉ MAP P80, D2

☎ 05 56 94 30 50

place Meynard

bell tower adult/child €5/3.50, free 1st Sun of month Sep-Jun

🕐 basilica 2-6pm Tue-Fri, bell tower 10am-1pm & 2-6pm Apr-Oct

Stained Glass

Bombing raids during WWII destroyed the church's magnificent stained-glass windows – those in the **Chapelle de Mons** are the only original windows to remain – but the modern stained-glass crafted in the 1960s casts the basilica interior in an impressive, dazzling rainbow of light on sunny days.

Side Chapels

In the 14th and 15th centuries, wealthy families and brotherhoods undertook the construction of 17 side chapels in the church, each dedicated to a different saint: plumbers and roofers prayed to St Suzanne, carpenters to St Joseph (hence the exquisitely carved altar and alabaster panels in the **Chapelle St-Joseph**), fishermen to St Fort, salt workers to St Roch, and so forth. In the **Chapelle Ste-Catherine,** dedicated to sailors, a beautiful statue of St Ursula evokes the 11,000 virgins who, according to legend, she was martyred with by the Huns in Cologne in 383AD.

Bell Tower

As with the city's cathedral, the bell tower or **Flèche St-Michel** stands apart from the basilica. Towering 114m tall, it is the second-highest tower in southern France and rewards those who stagger up its 230-odd steps with a magnificent city panorama.

Crypt

Beneath the belfry lies the basilica crypt, famous for its macabre collection of 70 mummies unearthed in a nearby cemetery in the 18th century and displayed here in their full glory until 1990. A short film instead recounts their ghoulish story to visitors today.

★ Top Tips

○ The basilica is only open in the afternoons; time your visit accordingly.

○ Scaling Flèche St-Michel is best on sunny, crystal-clear days when city views are second-to-none. The last climb up is 30 minutes before closing; note the bell tower is closed in winter.

○ Admission to the bell tower and crypt is free if you have a Bordeaux Métropole City Pass; otherwise, aim for the 1st Sunday of the month (September to June) when everyone can hike up its 230-odd steps for free.

✖ Take a Break

Grab a sandwich to go from La Boulangerie (p86) and picnic on a bench with basilica view on place Reynard.

For a first-class lunch of local fare to remember, reserve a table at La Tupina (p84).

Walking Tour 🚶

A Saturday Morning Market Stroll

The ancient market district of Capucins really comes to life on Saturday morning when locals roll out of bed and straight onto the streets to shop for their week's fruit and veg, catch up with friends over coffee or une verre (a glass of wine) and indulge in a long, lazy lunch as only the French can do.

Walk Facts
Start place des Capucins
End rue du Mirail
Length 2.5km; two hours

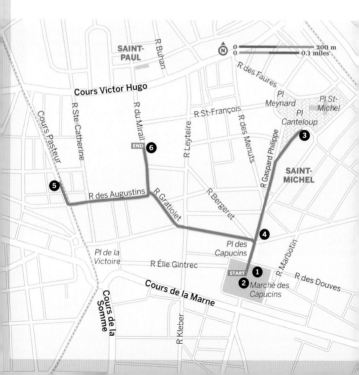

❶ Oysters for Breakfast

Arrive early to snag a plastic table between fruit and veg stalls at Chez Jean-Mi (p83). This iconic oyster bar inside the Capucins market is known all over the city for its superb oysters and copious seafood platters. Take the lead from locals propping up the bar and order a glass of dry white wine to accompany your breakfast feast.

❷ Market Meander

Belly full, allow ample time for browsing from market stall to stall inside the 'belly of Bordeaux,' as the historic Marché des Capucins (p89; 'Les Capus' to locals today) was known in the 19th century. Stalls selling all manner of fresh and dried produce, local and regional, have plied their trade here since the 1740s.

❸ Passage St-Michel

Meet Gilles, Samantha, Pierre and dozens of other local antique dealers at Passage St-Michel (p90), a covered flea market packed to the rafters with second-hand furniture, homewares, decorative objects, vintage clothing and pretty much anything else you can imagine.

❹ Au Bistrot

There is no finer spot for an authentic, market-driven lunch than Au Bistrot (p84), located just a hop and a skip from Marché des Capucins. Grab a petrol-blue bar stool at the bar and await your locavore feast of marinated herrings or lentil salad, roast pigeon or flambéed calf kidneys. Almost everything is sourced from local producers.

❺ A Pastry Class

Devote part of your Saturday to learning a new skill from locals: be it traditional Bordelais *canelé*, colourful macarons, stunning trompe l'œil fruit or basic cake design, Labo&Gato (p83) has all bases covered with its Saturday pastry classes.

❻ Crafting Beer

Should craft beer be your scene, enrol yourself on a Saturday afternoon beer-brewing workshop at L'Atelier Bière (p88) in Saint-Michel. Pick your own beer name and design your own label – and plot a return to Bordeaux a month later to pick up your home brew.

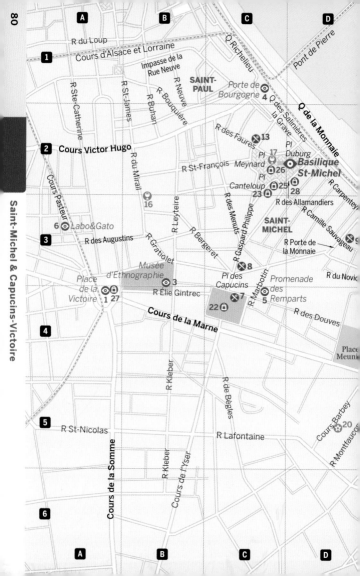

A
B
C
D

1

R du Loup

Cours d'Alsace et Lorraine

Q. Richelieu

Pont de Pierre

Impasse de la
Rue Neuve

SAINT-
PAUL

Porte de
Bourgogne ⊙ 4

Q des Salinières
la Grave

Q de la Monnaie

R Ste-Catherine

R St-James

R Buhan

R Neuve

R Bouquière

2

Cours Victor Hugo

R du Mirail

R St-François

R des Faures ✕ 13

Pl 17
Meynard ⊙
Pl 26
Canteloup
23 ⊙ 25

Pl Duburg
⊙ Basilique
St-Michel

R Carpenteye

Cours Pasteur

16

R Leyteire

R des Menuts

R Bergeret

R des Allamandiers

R Camille Sauvageau

SAINT-
MICHEL

9

3

6 ⊙ Labo&Gato

R des Augustins

R Gratiolet

R des Menuts

R Gaspard Philippe

R Porte de
la Monnaie

Musée
d'Ethnographie
⊙ 3

R Élie Gintrec

Pl des
Capucins

✕ 8

R Marbotin

Promenade
des
Remparts

R du Novic

Place
de la
Victoire ⊙ 1 27

✕ 7
22 ✕ ⊙ 5

R du Douves

Cours de la Marne

Place
Meuni

4

5

R St-Nicolas

R Kleber

R de Bègles

Cours Barbey

20

R Lafontaine

R Montfaucon

Cours de la Somme

R Kleber

Cours de l'Yser

6

A
B
C
D

E **F** **G** **H**

For reviews see

◉	Top Experiences	p76
◉	Sights	p82
✕	Eating	p83
🍷	Drinking	p87
✪	Entertainment	p88
🔒	Shopping	p89

0   400 m
0   0.2 miles

1
2
3
4
5
6

Garonne

Q des Queyries

Pont St-Jean

Q Sainte-Croix

15

10
2 Église Ste-
◉ Croix
Pierre
naudel

R des Étables

R Peyronnet

14

Q de la Palatade

Bvld des Frères Moga

R Charles Domercq

R de Tauzia

R St-Vincent de Paul

R Eugène le Roy

Gare de
Bordeaux-
Saint-Jean

R Furtado

R des Terres de Borde

R de Son-Tay

R La Seiglière

Place
Ferdinand
Buisson

18
19
21

✕ 12

Sights

Place de la Victoire

SQUARE

1 ◎ MAP P80, A4

The city's finest people-watching square, place de la Victoire throbs with students lingering over drinks on the vast cafe terraces here. Tray-wielding waitstaff dodge passing pigeons and buses, while children clamber on the bronze mother-and-baby turtles in the centre of the square. The sculpture (2005), by artist Ivan Theimer, stands beneath the **Colonne de la Victoire**, a marble obelisk by the same artist. Both works feature grapes as a celebration of Bordelais wine culture.

Église Ste-Croix

CHURCH

2 ◎ MAP P80, E3

Exquisite decorative sculptures representing greed, lust and other terrible age-old vices adorn the striking Romanesque façade of this elegant church in Ste-Croix. Built between the 11th and 12th centuries as the abbey church of an adjoining Benedictine abbey, this is Bordeaux's oldest church. The bell tower left of the main entrance was only added in the 19th century. Inside the original Dom Bedos pipe organ (1740–55) was moved to the cathedral in 1812. (place Pierre Renaudel; ⏲10am-6pm Mon-Fri)

Musée d'Ethnographie

MUSEUM

3 ◎ MAP P80, B3

A visit to this Museum of Ethnography is as much an excuse to nose around the old medical faculty of Bordeaux's prestigious university, established in 1441, as it is to admire the largely unsung collection of ethnographic treasures collected in Asia by Victor Segalen (1878–1919) – a French doctor from Brest studying naval medicine in Bordeaux – and other early explorers in the 19th and 20th centuries. (🕿05 57 57 18 97; https://meb.u-bordeaux.fr; 3ter place de la Victoire; admission free; ⏲2-6pm Mon-Thu, 10am-noon Fri)

Porte de Bourgogne

Porte de Bourgogne GATE

 MAP P80, C1

This Roman-style city gate
was designed in the 1750s by
18th-century celebrity architect
Ange-Jacques Gabriel (1698–
1782). Gabriel is best known for
redesigning Paris' place de la
Concorde, École Militaire and
the Petit Trianon at Versailles,
among other iconic buildings.
The gate marked the official
entrance into the city from Paris
and was renamed Porte Napoléon
in 1808 in honour of Napoleon's
visit to Bordeaux. It is sometimes
called Porte des Salinières after
the salt workers who lived in the
surrounding quarter. (place de
Bir Hakeim)

Promenade
des Remparts GARDENS

5 MAP P80, C4

An alley of centurion plane
trees charts out the course of
this elevated garden behind the
Capucins food market, built into
the remains of the 5km-long
city walls that protected the city
in the 14th century. The artil-
lery terraces, oratory and other
random architectural vestiges
littering the walkway were once
part of a 17th-century convent.
(8 rue Marbotin; admission free;
8.30am-8pm Jun-Aug, to 6.30pm
Mar-Apr, May, Sep & Oct, to 5.30pm
Nov-Feb)

Afternoon Treat:
Chocolatines 🍽

They are known as *pains au
chocolat* everywhere else in
France, but in Bordeaux the
classic French pastry filled
with strips of chocolate are
called *chocolatines*. In St-
Michel, La Boulangerie (p86)
sells one of the finest *chocolatines* going.

Labo&Gato COOKING

6 MAP P80, A3

An essential stop for every aspiring pastry chef, this down-to-earth
shop sells copper cake moulds
to make the city's signature
canelé (mini rum-and-vanilla
flavoured, sandcastle-shaped
cake) and an amazing choice of
tins, decorations and utensils
to bake the perfect Paris-Brest,
chateau-shaped birthday cake
etc. Its themed pastry, baking and
chocolate-making classes are the
best in town. (05 35 40 93 87;
https://atelierpatissier.laboetgato.fr;
61 cours Pasteur; 2-/4-hr class from
€40/60; 2-7pm Mon, 9am-7pm
Tue-Sat)

Eating

Chez Jean-Mi SEAFOOD €

7 MAP P80, C4

If there's one stall at the city's
iconic food market that sums up

Saint-Michel & Capucins-Victoire Eating

the contagious *joie de vivre* of Les Capus (as locals call the market), it is this *bistrot à huitres* (oyster bar). Jean-Mi greets regulars and first-timers with the same huge smile, and his freshly shucked oysters, fish soup and copious seafood platters are of the finest quality money can buy. (place des Capucins, Maré des Capucins; breakfast €1-7.50, seafood €6-25; ⏱7am-2.30pm Tue-Fri, to 3.30pm Sat & Sun)

Au Bistrot   FRENCH €€

8 ✕ MAP P80, C3

There's nothing flashy or fancy about this hardcore French bistro, an ode to traditional market cuisine with charismatic François front of house and talented French-Thai chef Jacques In'On in the kitchen. Marinated herrings, lentil salad topped with a poached egg, half a roast pigeon or a feisty *andouillette* (tripe sausage) roasted in the oven – 80% of produce is local or from the surrounding Aquitaine region. (☑06 63 54 21 14; www.facebook.com/aubistrotbordeaux; 61 place des Capucins; mains €18-24; ⏱noon-2.30pm & 7-11pm Wed-Sun)

Kuzina   GREEK €€

9 ✕ MAP P80, D3

Crete's Mediterranean kitchen is the inspiration for this casual eatery with bar-stool and shared-table seating. Select several *mezzés* (starters) such as beetroot and chickpea tzatziki, octopus salad and oysters, or opt for a set menu

incorporating lamb or veal chops. Vegetarians are well catered for and the *croustillant de féta aux fruits* (feta cheese and fruit pastry) ensures a deliciously sweet finale. (☑05 56 74 32 92; www.latupina.com; 22 rue Porte de la Monnaie; menus €17-27, mains €20; ⏱7-11pm Tue, noon-2pm & 7-11pm Wed-Sat)

Café du Théâtre   BISTRO €€

10 ✕ MAP P80, E3

What with the vintage three-wheeler parked on the peaceful square in front and the shaded terrace, the swish cafe-restaurant of the neighbouring theatre is a top lunch spot. Chef Hugo Lederer works with local, seasonal products to create his distinctive *cuisine du marché* (market cuisine) and his Saturday cooking classes (€120 including lunch) open with an atmospheric trip with him to the market. (☑05 57 95 77 20; www.le-cafe-du-theatre.fr; 3 place Pierre Renaudel; 2-/3-course lunch menu €20/27, mains €30-35)

La Tupina   FRENCH €€€

11 ✕ MAP P80, D3

Filled with the aroma of soup simmering inside a *tupina* ('kettle' in Basque) over an open fire, this iconic bistro is feted for its seasonal southwestern French fare: calf kidneys with fries cooked in goose fat, milk-fed lamb, tripe and goose wings. Dining is farmhouse-style, in a maze of small elegant rooms decorated

Dining à la Bordelaise

Local cuisine has its roots firmly tied to the *terroir* (land) while modern Bordeaux's innovative spirit bubbles over into the kitchen with young chefs occasionally casting away from the classics. In keeping with Bordeaux's staunchly locavore spirt, the best chefs work with fresh, seasonal ingredients from local farms or the nearby ocean: springtime asparagus, strawberries, black radishes, milk-fed Pauillac lamb, sturgeon caviar.

Mushrooms & Steak

The easiest way to dine local is simply to go for any tempting item on the menu that includes *à la Bordelaise* (Bordeaux) in its name. This said, there is no one straightforward interpretation of *à la Bordelaise* which means different things depending on the dish. *Cèpes à la Bordelaise* translates as some of France's finest mushrooms oven-baked in an earthenware dish with butter, garlic and the juice of green grapes. *Entrecôte à la Bordelaise,* more predictably, sees a feisty steak served with a rich red-wine sauce laced with shallots and herbs, while *escargots à la Bordelaise* are local snails cooked in tomatoes and white wine.

Oysters & Eels

No dish is more emblematic of Bordelaise cuisine than *lamproie à la bordelaise,* a devilishly unique dish starring slippery lampreys (a type of eel, practically prehistoric in appearance) that are fished in abundance in the nearby Gironde Estuary. Local myth says that when slaves in Burdigala (Roman Bordeaux) fell out of favour, the Romans fed them to the lampreys. A sucker fish, lampreys attach themselves to the bellies of other fish to feed on their blood. In the Bordeaux kitchen, they are chopped up into small pieces and slowly cooked over three successive days with leeks and spiced red wine. The resultant stew is traditionally conserved in jars, stored in the larder and eaten months later – in the honourable company, *bien sûr,* of a medium-aged St-Émilion or Pomerol red perhaps.

Bordeaux also has oysters, shoals of them, brought into market fresh each morning from nearby Arcachon and Cap Ferret. Not quite as exotic as they might sound, *huîtres à la Bordelaise* are simply freshly shucked oysters served on a bed of crushed ice, with hot *crépinettes* (little sausages) and a glass of fridge-cold, white Entre-deux-Mers.

Where to Eat & Drink

Eat Streets

Being the market 'hood that it is, eating options abound. There are several enticing traditional French bistros around the Capucins covered food market, and international quick eats – bagels, kebabs, Japanese, Thai, Indian, Sri Lankan, Moroccan, Vietnamese – jostle for attention along the southern end of pedestrian rue Ste-Catherine and in front of Basilique St-Michel on place Canteloup. Gourmets note: rue Porte de la Monnaie is the city's self-proclaimed 'rue gourmande'.

Café Central

Traditional cafes cluster around the market on place des Capucins. For a more tranquil moment with serene church view, grab a pew at a cafe terrace on pretty place Pierre Renaudel. Quai de Paludate, immediately south of Ste-Croix, is the night-owl hot spot for edgy late-opening bars, cocktails clubs and nightclubs.

with vintage photographs, antique furniture and silver tableware. (📞05 56 91 56 37; www.latupina.com; 6 rue Porte de la Monnaie; lunch menu €18, dinner menus €44-52, mains €20-32; ⏱noon-2pm & 7-11pm Tue-Sun)

Halle Boca   INTERNATIONAL €

12 ✕ MAP P80, H5

As part of the ambitious Euratlantique development project (p89), derelict abattoirs on the riverfront have been transformed into this state-of-the-art mall with dedicated space for pop-up events, a handful of casual eateries, and the fantastic La Boca Foodcourt with self-service beer wall, central cocktail and wine bar, and counters cooking seafood, traditional

Bordelais cuisine, pizza, gluten-free dishes et al. (http://halleboca.com; quai de la Palatade; ⏱8.30am-midnight Sun-Wed, 8.30am-11pm Thu, 8.30am-2am Fri & Sat)

La Boulangerie   SANDWICHES

13 ✕ MAP P80, C2

St-Michel's legendary bakery has been in the biz for over a century. House specialities include moist bread loaves studded with dried fruit, *escargots* (snail-shaped pastries specked with red fruit or chocolate and pistachio nuts) and *Jésuites* (custard-filled pastry iced with meringue and flaked almonds), and its made-to-order baguette sandwiches (pick three of dozens of fillings) ensure a lunchtime queue outside the door.

http://laboulangerie-saintmichel.fr;
9-51 rue des Faures; sandwiches €4-6;
⊙7am-7.30pm)

Drinking

Le Point Rouge   COCKTAIL BAR

4 🏠 MAP P80, F3

A black steel door marked with a
small, red doorbell (aka 'le point
rouge', or 'the red dot') heralds the
entrance to this trendy speakeasy,
a theatrical scarlet affair hidden in
the basement of a once-grandiose
riverfront *hôtel particulier* (mansion). The encyclopaedia of a
cocktail list traces the history
of cocktails including some 100
different elaborate creations. Ring
the bell to enter. (☏05 56 94 94 40;
www.pointrouge-bdx.com; 1 quai de
Paludate; ⊙6pm-2am Mon-Sat)

Le Taquin   COCKTAIL BAR

15 🏠 MAP P80, E3

Across from the river, by city
gate Porte de la Monnaie, serious
cocktails are shaken with style at
this hipster cocktail bar facing the
river. Steel-grey and baby-blue
chairs by Fermob inject a touch
of design and signature cocktails
ooze creativity: Clair de Lune rein-
vents the mojito with gin, litchi li-
queur and, *naturellement,* mounds
of fresh mint. Le Taquin serves excellent bistro fare (tasting platters
€10–15, mains €15–25) too. (☏05
56 78 97 10; https://letaquin.com; 1
quai Ste-Croix; ⊙noon-midnight Tue &
Thu-Sat, noon-6pm Wed)

Markets, Saint-Michel

The Classic Aperitif

In Bordeaux there is only one way to preempt the feast of a Bordelaise meal: with the local aperitif. Lillet is a delightfully pretty, salmon-pink aromatised wine from Podensac in the Graves wine-growing area. It mixes Bordeaux red, white or rosé wine with citrus liqueurs and is aged in barrels just like any other Bordeaux vintage. Drink it straight or on the rocks, with a lemon or orange wedge.

L'Atelier Bière   CRAFT BEER

16 🚇 MAP P80, B3

Enjoy a refreshing glass of *blanche* (white), *ambrée* (amber), *blonde* or *brune* (brown) beer brewed in situ at this innovative brasserie in Saint-Michel. A short tapas menu staves off hunger and true beer lovers can sign up for a beer-making workshop (from €90 for two hours, including 12 bottles of beer which you can only take a month later). (📞05 54 51 90 81; www.latelier-biere.com; 28 rue du Mirail; 🕑6pm-midnight Thu-Sat)

Au Bout du Monde   CAFE

17 🚇 MAP P80, C2

Lounge lizard-like in the sun over a pot of mint tea and honey-soaked Moroccan pastry at this popular neighbourhood cafe. Its pavement

terrace overlooks the spires of Basilica St-Michel. (📞05 56 91 46 43; 37 rue des Faures; 🕑8am-midnight Mon-Fri, 5pm-midnight Sat & Sun)

La Plage   CLUB

18 🚇 MAP P80, G4

Rocking it for a good couple of decades, La Plage (or The Beach) is an enormous nightclub with an imposing all-black façade on the quayside and several dance floors inside. DJs spin all sounds. Check its Facebook page for what's playing. (📞05 56 84 89 23; www.laplage-leclub.fr; 40 quai de Paludate; 🕑noon-6am)

La Pachanga   CLUB

19 🚇 MAP P80, G5

Spice up your life with a night of dancing at one of the many Caribbean-themed soirées at La Pachanga, a club playing tropical sounds, on club-hot quai de Paludate. (📞05 56 85 54 80; www.facebook.com/LaPachangadeBordeaux; 57bis quai de Paludate; 🕑midnight-7am Wed-Sat)

Entertainment

Rock School Barbey   LIVE MUSIC

20 ⭐ MAP P80, D5

Catch live bands at Rock School Barbey, funky host to a stream of up-and-coming French and international indie bands. Admission prices vary depending on the gig. And yes, this happening space eally is a rock school too. (☏05 56 3 66 00; www.rockschool-barbey; 8 cours Barbey; admission €10-25; ⏲hours vary)

e Port de la Lune JAZZ

1 ✪ MAP P80, H5

Check online for the line-up of gigs at this dark, atmospheric azz club. (☏05 56 49 15 55; www. ortdelalune-comptoirdujazz.com; 58 quai de la Paludate; ⏲7.30pm-2.30am Tue-Sat)

Shopping

Marché des Capucins MARKET

22 🅐 MAP P80, C4

A classic Bordeaux experience is a Saturday morning spent slurping oysters and white wine from a seafood stand in the city's legendary covered food market. Stalls overflowing with fruit, veg, cheese, meats, fish, bread and all sorts fill the space to bursting. (http://marchedescapucins.com; place des Capucins; ⏲6am-1pm Tue-Sun)

Bordeaux's New Quartier: Euratlantique

Take a walk on the wild side behind Gare St-Jean and you risk stumbling into a futuristic *quartier*. A maze of cranes and urban planners have been beavering away on the reconstruction of the riverbank wasteland between the central train station and the water. Euratlantique (www.bordeaux-euratlantique.fr) forms an entirely new business and residential district, with dazzling glass-and-steel office towers, eco-smart skyscrapers, long-derelict abattoirs upcycled as shopping malls, and a luxurious hotel. A steel bridge, the €125 million Pont Jean-Jacques Bosc, links the new left-bank 'hood to the right bank, with a radically vast section of it reserved exclusively for pedestrians and cyclists to promenade at leisure. All told, the mammoth project created around 30,000 jobs and homes for 40,000 inhabitants.

Méca, or Maison de l'Économie Créative et de la Culture (House of Creative Economy & Culture), is a staggering *grand projet* of an arts centre and incubator on the Euratlantique waterfront. The architecture alone is mind-blowing. Inside, regional cultural agencies, creative sectors and art-loving locals will share the same space to create a groundbreaking mecca for arts in Bordeaux. Along with studios and incubators for some of the region's most talented young artists, the new Méca hosts exhibition spaces, conference rooms, cinemas, a film studio, and a restaurant and cafe terrace.

Yvonne
CONCEPT STORE

23 🏠 MAP P80, C2

A lifestyle space dedicated to *l'art de vivre* (the art of living well) is the essence of this beautiful concept store and casual eatery in St-Michel. Its designer interior oozes style, as does the choice of tableware items, jewellery, homeware and gourmet foodstuffs, all curated with much thought and care by creative owner Isabelle. (☎ 05 56 72 19 16; www.yvonnelifestore.com; 2 rue Gaspard Philippe; ⏰ 11am-7pm)

L'Atelier de Lutherie
ARTS & CRAFTS

24 🏠 MAP P80, E3

Watch master luther Simon Bour at work in his beautiful workshop, filled to bursting with violins, violas and other elegant string instruments in front of Église Ste-Croix. The talented crafter trained in Cremona in Italy and his knowledge is second-to-none. (☎ 05 57 95 60 64; www.simonbour.com; 11bis place Pierre Renaudel; ⏰ 1.30-6.30pm Tue-Fri, 10am-noon & 1.30-6pm Sat)

Passage St-Michel
ANTIQUES

25 🏠 MAP P80, C2

Its claim to be an *'incubateur de tendances'* (trend incubator) might be a tad exaggerated, but rummaging through the stalls of some 20 secondhand dealers in this covered flea market is a colourful experience. Be it vintage furniture, decorative pieces, old boots, a wine vat or antiques you're after, you might well find it here. (☎ 05 56 74 01 84; www.lesbrocanteursdupassage. fr; 14 place Canteloup; ⏰ 9am-3pm Mon, 10am-6pm Tue-Sat)

Brocante du Dimanche
MARKE

26 🏠 MAP P80, C2

Sunday morning is the time to browse market stalls for antiques, vintage curiosities and a mindboggling array of unexpected bric-a-brac on the adjoining twinset of squares surrounding Basilica St-Michel. A smaller Marché Brocante (Flea Market) fills the same squares on Tuesday, Thursday and Friday mornings. The markets are a 700m walk downriver from the city centre. (Antique Market; place Meyard & place Canteloup; ⏰ 7am-2pm Sun)

Passage St-Michel

Marché des Bouquinistes

MARKET

7 🔒 MAP P80, A4

Bookworms linger longer than usual on place de la Victoire on Friday during the weekly secondhand book market. (place de la Victoire; ◷7am-6pm Fri)

Les Hangars

ANTIQUES

8 🔒 MAP P80, D2

Behind Basilica St-Michel, secondhand dealers sell their vintage wares – furniture, homewares, clothing, decorative objects – in an old recycled warehouse. (📞05 56 91 38 43; www.leshangars.com; 20 & 22 rue des Allamandiers; ◷9.30am-6pm Mon-Sat, 9am-2pm Sun)

Bordeaux's Market Mecca

No part of Bordeaux is as rich in open-air street markets: makeshift stalls, selling antiques, vintage curiosities and an eclectic choice of bric-a-brac, dot the basilica-shaded twinset of place Reynard and place Canteloup on Tuesday, Thursday, Friday and Sunday mornings. Arrive early to score the best bargains, bring your own shopping bag and watch your pockets – the markets do attract pickpockets and the occasional unsavoury type.

Walking Tour 🥾

Exploring La Bastide

Across the river, in downtown Bordeaux, the Rive Droite (Right Bank) was a wasteland until 1822 when it became linked to Rive Gauche (Left Bank) by the 17 stone arches of Pont de Pierre (1822). All too soon, the neighbourhood known as La Bastide buzzed with urban activity. Its mascot: a gargantuan blue lion by contemporary Lyonnais artist Xavier Veilhan on place de Stalingrad.

Getting There

Rive Droite is a 10-minute walk from place de Bir Hakeim on the Left Bank.

🚊 Line A eastbound from Hôtel Ville to Stalingrad or Jardin Botanique.

⛴ B³ boat from Les Hangars to Stalingrad.

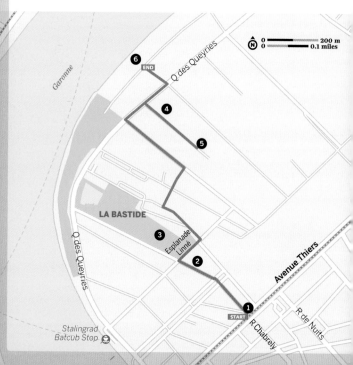

1 Église Ste-Marie de la Bastide

Every self-respecting *quartier* needs its own **church** (62 ave Thiers; admission free; ⏰hours vary), hence this elegant neo-medieval one from 1884. Upon first glance at its bulbous stone dome crowned by an elegant lantern on balusters, don't be surprised if Paris' Basilica de Sacré-Cœur in Montmartre comes to mind: the same architect, Paul Abadie (1812–84), designed both.

2 Le Bistrot du Caillou

Grab *un café* on the terrace of this local **hangout** (📞06 85 99 32 42; Esplanade Linné; ⏰noon-2.30pm Tue, noon-2.30pm & 7pm-midnight Wed-Sat), named after the curvaceous Teletubbies-styled bunker resembling an oversized *caillou* (pebble) in which it squats.

3 Jardin Botanique

Indulge in a green meander through the city's **Jardin Botanique de la Bastide** (📞05 56 52 18 77; http://jardin-botanique-bordeaux.fr; quai des Queyries; ⏰8am-8pm summer, to 6pm winter, greenhouses & exhibition hall 11am-6pm Tue-Sun), botanical gardens with a water garden showcasing stunning lilies, a vertical garden planted with vines and Mediterranean greenhouses.

4 Magasin Général

Lunch with Bordelais hipsters in France's largest organic **restaurant** (📞05 56 77 88 35; www.magasingeneral.camp; 87 quai des Queyries; mains €10-20; ⏰8am-6pm Mon, to 7pm Tue & Wed, to midnight Thu & Fri, 8.30am-midnight Sat, 8.30am-6pm Sun; 📶) with a terrace so large it sports several sofas, a ping-pong table and table football. Inside, vintage curiosities mix with 1950s formica tables, an organic *épicerie* (grocery), artisan beer brewery and coffee roaster.

5 Explore Darwin

At **Darwin** (📞09 53 01 86 22; www.hangardarwin.org; 87 quai des Queyries; €5; ⏰4-9pm Tue, Thu & Fri, 2-7pm Wed, Sat & Sun, 2-7pm Tue-Sun during school holidays; 🚊Maréchal Niel, 🚊Place Stalingrad) military barracks have been transformed into a green creative hub. Magasin Général occupies one hangar, and neighbouring hangars host a flea market, recycling stations, bike-repair workshop, urban farm, and skate park packed with riders at weekends.

6 Riverside Drinking & Dancing

Hit the riverbanks for after-dark dancing beneath fairy lights at **La Guinguette Chez Alriq** (📞05 56 86 58 49; www.laguinguettechezalriq.com; quai des Queyries; admission €5; ⏰7pm-11.30pm Wed, 7pm-midnight Thu & Fri, 5pm-1.30am Sat, noon-7pm Sun May-Sep). Sip homemade punch and artisan beer brewed at Bordeaux's Brasserie de la Lune. *Santé!*

Explore

Saint-Seurin & Fondaudège

Elegant and discrete, Saint-Seurin and Fondaudège offer a snapshot of bourgeois Bordeaux. Wealthy wine merchants and industrialists chose this quiet residential neighbourhood to build sumptuous mansions in the 18th and 19th centuries and their legacy lingers in a bespoke scattering of lavish chateaux and hôtels particuliers (private mansions). But scratch the surface and fascinating relics of Gallo-Roman civilisation and ancient Christian martyrdom emerge, not to mention a burgeoning foodie scene.

Begin on place Gambetta. Grab un café gourmand (coffee and sweet treats) at Baillardran (p101), then head north to Basilique St-Seurin (p96). Continue the history theme with a stroll to Palais Gallien (p102) to admire the only remaining vestiges of Roman Bordeaux. Afterwards, enjoy a gourmet lunch at a fashionable eatery on rue du Palais Gallien or rue Lafaurie de Monbadon. Devote the afternoon to exploring the northern part of the 'hood: the Jardin Public (p103), Natural History Museum (p103) and memorable Institut Culturel Bernard Magrez (p101).

Getting There & Around

🚊 **Tram** Line B two stops southbound from Esplanade des Quinconces to the Gambetta stop; line C northbound from Gare St-Jean to Jardin-Public.

Neighbourhood Map on p100

Porte Dijeaux, place Gambetta (p102) IVO ANTONIE DE ROOIJ/SHUTTERSTOCK ©

Top Experience 📷

Stop in at Pilgrimage Site Basilique St-Seurin

The soul of Saint-Seurin lies in this sacred Roman-esque complex, built from the 11th century on top of an ancient Gallo-Roman necropolis. Medieval pilgrims following the Way of St James made it a key stop on their southbound route to Santiago de Compostela in Spain. The basilica was inscribed as a historical monument in 1840 and gained Unesco World Heritage status in 1998.

◉ MAP P100, B4

📞 05 56 48 22 08

www.saintseurin.info

place des Martyrs et de la Résistance

admission free

🕓 8.30am-7.45pm Tue-Sat, 9am-8.15pm Sun

Architecture

The basilica's neo-Romanesque facade was designed by architect Pierre-Alexandre Poitevin in 1828, with Italian sculptor Dominique Fortuné Maggesi (1801–92) creating the many decorative statues and exuberant stone ornamentation.

Saint Severinus

The basilica is named after the patron saint of Bordeaux and the city's fourth bishop, Saint Seurin (or Saint Severinus in English). Read the story of the saint in 14 scenes sculpted in alabaster on the main altar and give a nod of respect to his sarcophagus safeguarded here. Only 32 of the original 47 beautifully carved, wooden choir stalls from the 15th century remain.

Chapels

In the 14th and 15th centuries the basilica was enlarged with several side chapels, although **Chapelle Notre Dame de Bonne Nouvelle**, with an exquisite 14th-century alabaster statue of the Virgin believed to be miraculous, is the only one to retain its medieval appearance. Left of the choir, **Chapelle Notre Dame de la Rose** is a superb example of Flamboyant Gothic architecture with an altarpiece from 1444 illustrating the life of the Virgin Mary in 12 scenes.

Crypt

Stairs lead down from the nave to the tiny but atmospheric crypt, filed with marble sarcophagi of early bishops. The **tomb of Saint Fort**, believed to be the first bishop of Bordeaux, is also here. Traditionally, on 16 May each year, Bordelaise mothers would bring their sons to the tomb in order to make men of (aka 'fortify') their young sons.

★ **Top Tips**

o The basilica offers free guided visits at 2pm Saturday year-round, plus 4pm Sunday in summer.

o In July and August the tourist office organises atmospheric after-dark guided tours of the Archaeological Site, departing at 9.30pm Thursday (€5); reserve in advance online or at the tourist office.

o Extend your visit with a meander around the basilica's neighbouring Site Archéologique de St-Seurin (p101); the archeological site is open afternoons only from June to September; plan accordingly.

✕ **Take a Break**

Take a coffee break over a finely roasted espresso or homemade ginger lemonade at Le Monologue (p107).

Walking Tour 🥾

Flânerie in Bourgeois Bordeaux

*For aspiring flâneurs (strollers) keen to indulge
in local vibe rather than serial sightseeing, there
is no finer neighbourhood. Exploring mellow
Saint-Seurin is all about savouring its distinctive
bourgeois airs and graces at a delicious
go-slow pace.*

Walk Facts
Start place Gambetta
End rue Labottière
Length 4km; two hours

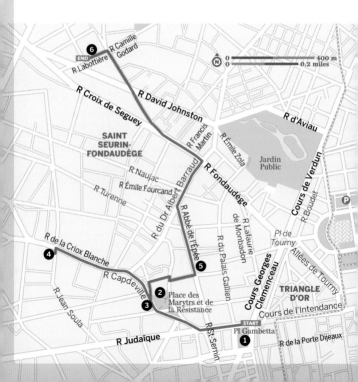

❶ Place Gambetta

Begin on this large open square (p102), Bordeaux's exact geographic centre in the 19th century when the stone roadside marker marking *point zéro* was placed in front of No 10. Stroll at leisure – the essence of French *flânerie* – around the leafy square, soaking up its elegant line-up of 18th-century townhouses.

❷ Place des Martyrs et de la Résistance

Walk west along rue Judaïque to this beautiful square, dominated by the Romanesque hulk of Basilique St-Seurin (p96). On townhouse facades, keep an eye out for *mascarons* – decorative masks inspired by the Renaissance and all the rage among 18th-century Bordelais architects who often chose Bacchus, God of wine, as the inspiration behind these stone-sculpted faces.

❸ Hôtel Frugès

Eye-catching Hôtel Frugès at No 63 was built in 1878 but renovated in an eclectic, art deco/nouveau style from 1913 by industrialist Henri Frugès who made his fortune refining sugar. A passionate art lover, he employed the finest artists and artisans of the day to 'modernise' the mansion with wrought-iron balconies, a loggia, top-floor rotunda, bow windows, decorative stained-glass, ceramics, paintings and stone friezes.

❹ Rooftop Cats

Weave your way down narrow lanes to rue Jean Soula where, at No 109, a sitting cat peers down on you from the rooftop. Watch your back for other decorative stone cats by French architect Jean-Jacques Valleton (1841–1916) in this feline-friendly neighbourhood.

❺ Yndō Hôtel

Break for coffee and a sneak peek at contemporary art, including edgy wall murals by Bordeaux artist Yannick Fournié, at **Yndō Hôtel** (https://yndohotelbordeaux.fr; 108 rue Abbé de l'Épée), at home in an 18th-century *hôtel particulier*.

❻ Château Labottière

Count 20 minutes of pleasant *flânerie* to reach the ultimate stop: yet more fantastic contemporary art at the Institut Culturel Bernard Magrez (p101), at home in impossibly romantic, 18th-century Château Labottière.

2 Institut Culturel Bernard Magrez

R Labottière

R David Johnston

20

R Croix de Seguey

N 0 ——— 200 m
0 ——— 0.1 miles

R d'Avia

R St-Laurent

R Émile Zola

Musée Bordeaux – Sciences et Nature

R Naujac

Palais Gallien

5
9

8

7 Jardin Public

R Sansas

16

R Émile Fourcand

19

Maison du Tourisme de la Gironde

R Turenne

R du Palais Gallien

R Lafaurie de Monbadon

R Fondaudège

Cours de V

SAINT-SEURIN-FONDAUDÈGE

R Turenne

R du Dr Albert Barraud

R Abbé de l'Épée

R Lebrun

11

21

R Huguerie

R Condillac

10

R Capdeville

Basilique St-Seurin

Le Boutique Hôtel

TRIANG D'OR

12

R Rolland

Cours Georges Clemenceau

Site Archéologique de St-Seurin

3

R Castéja

17

14 18

Cours de l'Intendant

1

15

6 Place Gambetta

R Judaïque

Café Baillardran

4

Piscine Judaïque

Centre Commercial Mériadeck

R du Château d'Eau

R St-Sermin

R des Remparts

R Bouffard

R Boulan

R Montbazon

Jardin de la Mairie

Pl Jean Moulir

Esplanade Charles de Gaulle

R Élisée Reclus

R du Maréchal Joffre

R Jean Fleuret

13

Cours du Maréchal Juin

R de Belfort

R Ligler

Cours d'Albret

R du

Sights

Baillardran COOKING

◉ MAP P100, C4

Not to be missed is a cookery class (two hours, €49–65 including tasting) to learn how to make *canelés* at the École du Canelé, inside this Bordeaux-chic pastry shop. The mini sandcastle-shaped *canelé,* the city's most famous cake, is baked in a copper mould, has a moist centre and caramelised crust, and is flavoured with a dash of vanilla and rum.

Baillardran is also a sweet spot between shops for indulging in a *café gourmand,* aka an espresso or white coffee with a sweet macaron, nougatine stick and signature *canelé* on the side. (☑ 09 67 79 52 74; www.baillardran.com; 36 place Gambetta; ⏱ 8am-8pm Mon-Sat, 9am-6.30pm Sun)

Institut Culturel Bernard Magrez GALLERY

◉ MAP P100, A1

Glittering glass chandeliers, parquet flooring, original moulded ceilings and pretty peppermint-green painted wood-panelling create a wonderfully romantic backdrop for the compelling contemporary-art exhibitions held at Château Labottière. The neoclassical chateau was constructed in 1773 for Bordelais brothers Antoine and Jacques Labottière who ran a small printing business in Bordeaux and is owned today by

Point Zéro

Bordeaux's *point zéro,* from which all distances in France to the city are measured, is located right here in the 'hood on place Gambetta. Begin your neighbourhood explorations by finding your bearings on this central square – Casablanca is 1385km south, Riga 2174km northeast.

the Bernard Magrez cultural institute. (Château Labottière; ☑ 05 56 81 72 77; www.institut-bernard-magrez. com; 16 rue de Tivoli; adult/child €8/ free, free 1st Sun of month; ⏱ 1-6pm Fri-Sun)

Site Archéologique de St-Seurin ARCHAEOLOGICAL SITE

3 ◉ MAP P100, B4

Not to be confused with the small crypt inside Basilique St-Seurin (p96), this archaeological site was uncovered in 1910 when archaeologists excavated part of the vast Christian necropolis beneath place des Martyrs et de la Résistance.

Today, you can descend into its dimly lit depths to admire tombstones dating from the 4th to 18th century, medieval frescoes, amphorae and other ancient relics.

Legend says Charlemagne buried many of his loyal knights here, after they were lost in battle at Roncevaux Pass in 778 after Basque troops ambushed Charlemagne's army on the

Pyrenean mountain pass. (☏05 56 00 66 08; place des Martyrs de la Résistance; admission free; ☉1-6pm Jun-Sep)

Piscine Judaïque SWIMMING

4 ◉ MAP P100, A5

This beautiful art-deco pool first opened its doors in 1936. One of the two indoor pools has a retractable roof and there's a spa, kid-friendly slide and generous sprinkling of sun-loungers. Swimming hats and speedos (men, no Bermuda shorts *s'il vous plaît*) are obligatory. (☏05 56 51 48 31; 164 rue Judaïque; adult/child €4.95/3.55; ☉hours vary Tue-Sun, to 9.30pm Thu)

Palais Gallien RUIN

5 ◉ MAP P100, C2

It was Celtic tribes who first established Bordeaux, but it wasn't until about 200 years later, under the rule of the Romans, that the town started to blossom. Back then it was called Burdigala; today the only remains of Burdigala are the crumbling ruins of this 3rd-century amphitheatre. (rue du Dr Albert Barraud; admission free)

Place Gambetta SQUARE

6 ◉ MAP P100, C4

The old street plaques – place Dauphiné and place Nationale – remain firmly on the wall of one building as a reminder of this tree-shaded square's colourful

Palais Gallien

Charlemagne in Bordeaux

Legend says that Charlemagne buried many of his loyal knights in the Christian necropolis beneath place des Martyrs et de la Résistance (today the Site Archéologique de St-Seurin, p101), lost in battle at Roncevaux Pass in 778 after Basque troops ambushed Charlemagne's army on the Pyrenean mountain pass. It was after the same battle that Charlemagne laid the ivory horn blown by his courageous nephew, Roland, on the altar in the basilica (Seurin even gets a mention in the famous medieval French epic poem *La Chanson de Roland*). The precious relic, venerated for centuries by pilgrims, remained in Basilica St-Seurin until the French Revolution when the church was sacked and the horn lost.

...ast. Framed by elegant 18th-
...entury buildings, the square fell
...utside the original city walls –
...hich perhaps makes it all the
...ore ironic that Bordeaux's *point
...ero*, the geographic centre of
...e city in the 19th century from
...hich all distances from Bor-
...eaux are measured, lies in this
...quare. A stone marker outside 10
...ace Gambetta marks the exact
...oint.

Jardin Public   GARDENS

 MAP P100, D2

...andscaping is artistic as well as
...formative at the Jardin Public.
...stablished in 1755 and laid out in
...e English style a century later,
...e grounds incorporate duck
...onds, the meticulously cata-
...gued **Jardin Botanique** dating
...om 1629, and the city's Musée
...ordeaux – Sciences et Nature.
...ours de Verdun)

Musée Bordeaux – Sciences et Nature   MUSEUM

8 ⊙ MAP P100, D2

With more than one million different specimens on show, Bordeaux's former Natural History Museum is among France's most impressive. It is housed in the elegant Hôtel de Lisleferme (1780) in the city's stunning flower-festooned Jardin Public.

The modern museum uses interactive exhibits and digital displays to excellent effect. On the ground floor, children aged six and under can enjoy their own dedicated Musée des Tout-Petits. (☎05 24 57 65 30; www.museum-bordeaux.fr; 5 place Bardineau; adult/child €5/3, with temporary exhibition €7/5)

Eating

Mets Mots
BISTRO €€

9 🗺 MAP P100, C2

Talented young chef Léo Forget is turning heads in foodie Bordeaux with his striking locavore neobistro, with stylish zinc bar, mix of rough chip-wood and retro geometric-tile flooring and a back wall plastered in faded ginger newspapers.

The lunchtime *menu,* which might see *confit de canard* (confit duck) with old-world veg or sweet-and-sour cod chalked on the board, is unbeatable value. (📞 05 57 83 38 24; www.metsmots.fr; 98 rue Fondaudège; 2-/3-course lunch menu from €19/23, 3-/4-/5-course dinner menu €34/45/65; ⊙noon-1.30pm Mon, noon-1.30pm & 7.30-9.30pm Tue-Fri)

Nama
FUSION €

10 🗺 MAP P100, D3

A refreshingly creative, Franco-Japanese cuisine is cooked up by the duo of chefs at this street-smart restaurant with age-old exposed stone walls and contemporary decor. The menu might include seafood *pot au feu* (stew), beef tartare or pork marinated in sweet spices, and the playful wine list pitches Bordeaux vintages against New World wines. (📞 05 56 44 88 54; www.namawinerestaurant.com; 24 rue Lafaurie Monbadon; 3-/4-/5-course menu €36/42/52; ⊙7.30-11.30pm Tue-Sun)

Canelés

Bordelais Sweet Treats 🍽

Canelés

It is said that Bordeaux's signature cake – the tiny, sandcastle-shaped *canelé* – was first cooked by frugal nuns in the 16th century who scraped up spilled flour from the quaysides and mixed it with the dozens of egg yolks going spare (the whites were used to clarify the red wine) and a splash of cheap rum from the colonies to make cakes for the poor. True or not, the bite-size cake is frequently served with coffee at the end of a meal or as as *goûter* (the traditional afternoon snack) and is found all over Bordeaux today. Cooking classes at iconic Bordelaise patisserie, Baillardran (p101), still use the traditional, shiny copper moulds. The perfect *canelé* is crunchy and caramelised on the outside but creamy like set custard inside.

Cherry Soup

One of Bordeaux's most fantastic desserts, *soupe aux cerises au vin de Bordeaux* sees fresh plump cherries cooked in local red wine with sugar, vanilla and star anise. Once boiling, the soup is instantly removed from the heat and left to rest for three days. The resultant wine-buxom cherries are sublime. *Le Millas* is another equally old dessert, baked in many a chateau kitchen with eggs, sugar, flour and milk subtly perfumed with lemon zest or almond.

Sweets & Biscuits

A *Bouchon de Bordeaux* is not a traditional *bouchon* (cork; still used across the board by Bordeaux winemakers) but a bite-sized pastry filled with an explosive combo of almond paste and candied grapes macerated in Fine de Bordeaux grape brandy.

Other sweet treats include *Dunes Blanches* (puffs of choux pastry filled with an unusual vanilla-dashed whipped cream) and macaron biscuits containing just egg whites and almonds from nearby St-Émilion. In the medieval village, macaron biscuits by 1930s biscuit workshop **Nadia Fermingier** (📞05 57 24 72 33; www.macarons-saint-emilion.fr; 9 rue Guadet; 🕔8am-7pm Mon-Sat, 9am-7pm Sun) are reckoned to be the best (albeit the priciest).

Fanchonnettes Bordelaises are oval boiled sweets filled with almonds, chocolate, coffee or fruit pulp. They were created in the 19th century by a pair of music-loving sisters who named their bonbon after a singer called Fanchon who lived on their street.

A Cake for Kings

On 6 January (Epiphany), to celebrate the Three Wise Men arriving in Jerusalem to pay homage to the infant Jesus, much gaiety is had around the family table with a *galette des Rois*. A puff-pastry tart filled with frangipane in the rest of France, the Bordelaise 'cake for kings' is a crown-shaped ring of brioche studded with candied fruits and sugar crystals. Recipe aside, the game remains the same. Who will bite into the single *fève* (literally 'the bean') hidden inside the tart? Whoever does is crowned king with a gold paper crown sold with the galette. 'The bean' these days translates as a thumb-sized porcelain miniature. In keeping with the local spirit of things, one Bordelais *pâtisserie* recently produced 14 different *fèves* to collect, each a miniature of a different famous Bordeaux monument.

Baud et Millet
CHEESE €€

11   MAP P100, D3

If you like cheese or wine, or both, then this unassuming neighbourhood bistro strung with tin milk churns is gold. It serves more than 100 different cheeses in myriad forms, alongside almost as many wines. Curious *fromage* lovers should indulge in a seasonal oven-baked Mont d'Or, only available October to March.

End with a cherry- and chocolate-laced mousse made with goat cheese from the Pyrenees. (205 56 79 05 77; 19 rue Huguerie; mains €18-40; noon-2pm & 7-9.30pm Mon-Sat)

Drinking

Le Monologue
COFFE

12   MAP P100, C4

Every fashionable city street has to have one – a new-generation coffee shop, that is – and on rue du Palais Gallien it's Le Monologu Green-floral wallpaper and plush, velour zig-zag cushions by Parisia design house Maison de Vacances bathe the interior in urban cool. Front-of-house Lyonnaise gal Morgane is full of smiles. (205 54 49 93 12; www.facebook.com/le monologuebordeaux33; 35 rue du Palais Gallien; 9am-6pm Tue-Fri, 11am-4pm Sun)

Café Gusco

COFFEE

3 🕓 MAP P100, C6

From the miniature bouquets of dried flowers wedged in coffee beans in glass vases on the tables to the peppermint-green walls and wicker lampshades, very last detail is taken great care of at this specialist coffee shop. Pauline – Bordeaux's only female roaster and barista – is the creative force behind it all. Her lunchtime tarts are equally superb. A picture-postcard terrace beneath trees rounds off the enchanting ensemble. (📞 06 10 37 9 29; www.cafegusco.com; 2 rue Li-ier; 🕓 8am-2.30pm Mon, 8am-6pm ue-Fri, 9am-noon Sat; 🛜)

Koeben

COFFEE

14 🕓 MAP P100, C4

Coffee shop, tea room, upmarket grocery and design-cool boutique: overnight this Scandinavian drink-dine-shop hybrid upped the street cred of fashionable rue du Palais Gallien. The interior is predictably clean-cut, with a muted colour palette, pale wood flooring and Danish-designed furniture of course. In the kitchen owner Peter Johansen prepares recipes inspired by his Danish mother's cook book.

Look forward to marinated herrings, salmon, lots of black bread and a must-try Sunday brunch (adult/child €33/17). (www.facebook.com/koeben33; 32 rue du

ordelais *galette des Rois*

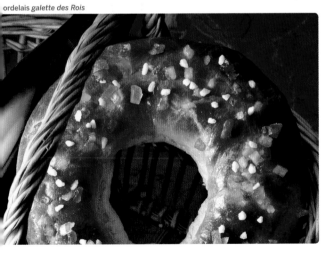

Palais Gallien; ⊙9am-7pm Tue-Sat, 11.30-3.30pm Sun)

Sherlock Holmes PUB

15 🚌 MAP P100, C4

With a handful of alfresco tables down a side alley and ample bar seating inside, this faithfully traditional British pub lures a pint-happy crowd. Darts, the odd pub quiz, live sports on the big screen, board games and authentic English beer shipped from Bedford's Eagle Brewery to Bordeaux provide the usual entertainment. (📞05 56 48 51 22; www.sherlockholmespub.fr; 16 rue Judaïque; ⊙4pm-2am Mon-Fri, 2pm-2am Sat, 2pm-1am Sun)

L'Orangerie CAF

16 🚌 MAP P100, D2

In warm and sunny weather, flop out on an orange deckchair at the Orangerie, an attractively located cafe (best for simple drinks rather than food) with generous pavement terrace in the flowery Jardin Public (p103).

Find it right next to the eastern city park entrance on cours de Verdun. (📞05 56 48 24 41; www.lorangeriedebordeaux.com; cours de Verdun, Jardin Public; ⊙7am-9pm Jun-Aug, shorter hours rest of year; 👫)

Jardin Public (p103)

Historic Bordeaux: The Celts to Charlemagne

Burdigala

The Bituriges Vivisci, a Celtic tribe, settled on swampy marshland around the mouth of the tiny Devèze River – a left-bank tributary of the Garonne – in the 4th century BCE. The city fell under Roman rule from around 60 BCE and quickly emerged as a hub of tin and lead trading in the Roman Empire. The first vines were planted. Magnificent temples, baths, an aqueduct and an amphitheater were constructed; a glass scale model in Bordeaux's Musée d'Aquitaine shows the 20,000-seat arena – today ruins in Saint-Seurin known as Palais Gallien – in its Roman heyday.

In the 3rd century CE Burdigala became the capital of Roman Aquitaine. Ramparts were constructed around the city in 271 CE, and ancient grave headstones (found today in the Musée d'Aquitaine) of traders from far-flung spots in the Roman Empire, used as foundations in the ramparts, show just how prosperous and cosmopolitan Roman Burdigala was. Wine from here, transported in distinctive flat-bottomed ceramic amphorae, was purportedly even served at the emperor's table in Rome.

Bordeaux in the Middle Ages

The collapse of the Roman Empire opened the floodgates to a wave of invasions by the Vandals, Visigoths, Franks and other Germanic tribes from the north.

The newfangled faith of Christianity arrived in the region, churches were built, and the first pilgrims en route to Santiago de Compostela in Spain rolled into town.

In 778, following the disastrous Battle of Roncevaux Pass, when Basque troops ambushed the army of Charlemagne on a high mountain pass in the nearby Pyrenees, Charlemagne laid many of his loyal knights to rest in Église St-Seurin, the city's oldest church built on top of a Gallo-Roman necropolis.

In the 11th century, the region fell into the hands of the Dukes of Gascony and later the Duke of Aquitaine.

Entertainment

La Grande Poste ARTS CENTRE

17 ⭐ MAP P100, C4

Admire the art-deco domed ceiling and original octagonal windows of this former post office, telephone and telegraph centre where Bordelais once queued to send messages via electrical signals.

Closed in the 1970s, it is now a groundbreaking *'espace improbable'* (improbable space) where people come to breakfast (€8.50), brunch and lunch (adult/child €25/12); catch a show; listen to live music or DJ sets; or browse pop-up boutiques. (📞05 56 01 53 90; www.lagrandeposte.com; 7 rue du Palais Gallien; ⏰9am-1am Tue-Sat, 11am-7pm Sun)

L'Auditorium CONCERT VENUE

18 ⭐ MAP P100, D4

Music concerts embracing all genres – classical, jazz, blues, world music, orchestral performances – take to the stage at this contemporary, glass-fronted concert hall run by Bordeaux's opera house. (📞05 56 00 85 95; www.opera-bordeaux.com; 9-13 cours Georges Clemenceau)

Marché de Lerme ARTS CENTRE

19 ⭐ MAP P100, B3

Occasional art exhibitions and cultural happenings are held in this former covered market hall, an eye-catching glass-and-iron

Sherlock Holmes pub (p108)

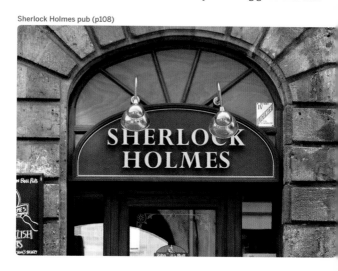

---

structure designed by architect Charles Buguet in 1866. (place de Lerme; ⏱hours vary)

Shopping

Cave Briau

WINE

20 🔒 MAP P100, B1

Not only does the wine sold at this fantastically well-stocked cellar cover the whole range of prices (read: €2.50 to €5000 a bottle), bottles are also arranged by price making it dead easy to head straight for the shelf that suits your budget. Choose from 500-odd references, sold at chateau prices. Twice a month the cellar runs wine-tasting classes. (📞05 56 79 25 71; www.briau.com; 94 rue David Johnston; ⏱9am-12.30pm & 2-7.30pm Mon-Sat)

Le Goût du Papier

ARTS & CRAFTS

21 🔒 MAP P100, C3

This concept store dedicated to all things paper – stationery, sculptures, books and toys – is wonderful to browse. Its weekend crafting workshops for adults (€25 to €28) and children (€15 to €18) explore scrapbooking, origami, garland-making, finger puppets,

Luxurious
Le Boutique

Blind wine tastings, Sunday brunch and concerts enliven the stylish tapas and wine bar inside **Le Boutique** (Map p100, D4; 📞05 56 48 80 40; https://hotelbordeauxcentre.com; 3 rue Lafaurie Monbadon), a luxurious four-star hotel in a beautiful 18th-century *hôtel particulier* (mansion).

kirigami and other paper crafts. Check its website for details. (📞05 57 83 71 94; www.legoutdupapier.com; 88 rue du Palais Gallien; ⏱11am-6pm Mon, 10am-7pm Tue-Sat)

Oliv'Art

FOOD

'Agitateur des Papilles' ('tastebud agitator') is the strapline of this tempting boutique (see 15 🔒 Map p100, C4), an upmarket grocery specialising in olive oils and vinegars from regional wineries. It sells oil-laced tapenades (dips) and sauces, biscuits and so on, too. (📞05 56 44 56 82; www.facebook.com/Olivart-Bordeaux; 4 rue Judaïque; ⏱2.30-7pm Mon, 10am-1.30pm & 2.30-7pm Tue-Sat)

Worth a Trip

St-Émilion

*Languishing among picture-postcard vineyards
famed for producing some of France's finest
full-bodied red wines, the medieval village of St-
Émilion is the Bordeaux region's most handsome
and magical wine town. An easy trip by train from
the city, it is well worth a day trip to taste the
exceptional wine in situ and explore its golden,
Unesco-listed old town.*

Getting There

🚌 St-Émilion is 47km east
of Bordeaux.

🚃 Gare St-Jean to
St-Émilion (€9.50, 35 minutes), then a 1.7km walk
to the village. Or beckon a
tuk-tuk.

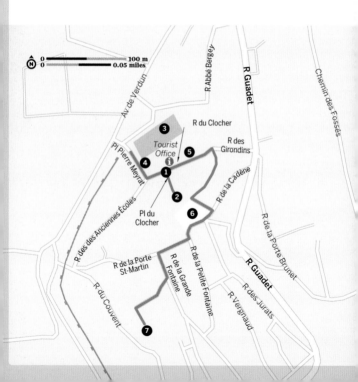

1 Alfresco Terrace People-Watching

Grab a coffee on **place du Clocher** and enjoy the bird's-eye view of the village's original market square. The **tourist office** (📞 05 57 55 28 28; www.saint-emilion-tourisme.com; place des Créneaux; ⏱ 9.30am-7.30pm Jul & Aug, shorter hours rest of year), in a 15th-century refectory, is on the same square.

2 Clocher de l'Église Monolithe

Grab a key from the tourist office and spiral up the 196-step staircase in **Clocher de l'Église Monolithe** (Bell Tower; place des Créneaux; €2; ⏱ 9.30am-7.30pm Jul & Aug, shorter hours rest of year), the Flamboyant Gothic belfry of Église Monolithe hollowed out of limestone rock in the 12th to 15th centuries. Vineyard views from the top are beautiful – spot Bordeaux.

3 Église Collégiale

To the right of the tourist office, an archway leads into the romantic cloister of the **Église Collégiale** (Collegiate Church; place Pierre Meyrat). Cross its full length to access the church, with a domed Romanesque 12th-century nave and almost-square vaulted choir dating to the 14th and 16th centuries.

4 A Lesson in Wine

Stumble out of the dimly lit church and straight into St-Émilion's hallowed **Maison du Vin de Émilion**

(📞 05 57 55 50 55; www.maisonduvin saintemilion.com; place Pierre Meyrat; ⏱ 9.30am-6.30pm May-Oct, 9.30am-12.30pm & 2-6pm Nov-Apr). Test your sense of smell with an exhibition on St-Émilion's different appellations and aromas, and allow a sommelier to guide you through a 40-minute blind tasting of three wines (€20) or grands crus (wines of exceptional quality; €28).

5 A Gourmet Lunch

Lunch at **L'Envers du Decors** (📞 06 57 74 48 31; www.envers-du decor.com; 11 rue du Clocher; mains €24-34; ⏱ noon-2.30pm & 7-10.30pm), an exceptional bistro cooking up Bordelais classics such as lamproie à la Bordelaise (a local eel-like fish simmered in red wine). The wine list is as sensational.

6 Place de l'Église Monolithique

Weave your way along the village's signature tertres (incredulously steep, narrow streets) to **place de l'Église Monolithique**, another enchanting medieval square.

7 La Tour du Roy

Hike up this sturdy **square tower** (rue du Couvent; adult/child €2/free; ⏱ 2-5.30pm Mon-Fri, 11am-12.15pm & 2-5.30pm Sat & Sun Jul & Aug, shorter hours rest of year, closed Jan) – the remains of a 13th-century donjon. At the top swoon over remarkable views of St-Émilion, the Dordogne River and its bucolic valley.

Explore ✦

Chartrons, Bassins à Flot & Bacalan

Dramatic contrasts between old and new seduce visitors in this fashionably bohemian quarter where Bordeaux's wine-trading history comes to life. Artist studios, antique galleries and independent boutiques pepper village-like Chartrons, named after Carthusian monks who lived here from 1383 until the 15th century when wine merchants moved in. Across the water, north of the Bassins à Flot (wet docks), cranes lace the skyline in regenerated 19th-century port district Bacalan.

Begin your day in Chartrons, hemmed in by 18th-century mansions on Pavé des Chartrons (p126). Visit the Musée du Vin et du Négoce (p124) and mooch antique malls on rue Notre Dame. Lunch at Bocca a Bocca (p129). Saunter north to the Bassins à Flot – wet docks cut off from the River Garonne by a lock – in marshland-turned-port Bacalan. Catch an exhibition at La Base Sous-Marine (p118), then hit La Cité du Vin (p116). End with wine tasting and dinner with view at Restaurant Le 7 (p129).

Getting There & Around

🚊 **Tram** Line B northbound from Gare St-Jean to Quinconces, then tram C along the river to the Chartrons or La Cité du Vin stops.

⛴ **Boat** B[3] (www.infotbm.com) link quai de Bacalan (by the Quai des Marques shopping mall and La Cité du Vin) with quai des Maréchal Lyautey (near Palais de la Bourse) and quay des Queyries on the right bank.

Neighbourhood Map on p122

Top Experience 📷

Taste World-Class Wines at La Cité du Vin

The groundbreaking City of Wine is an essential stop on any Bordeaux itinerary. Its insightful permanent exhibition and tasting workshops cover every aspect of wine imaginable and extend far beyond the vignobles (vineyards) of Bordeaux. The museum's architecture is just as sensory: its curvaceous gold building on the banks of the River Garonne resembles a wine decanter.

◎ **MAP P122, F3**

📞 05 56 16 20 20

www.laciteduvin.com

134-150 Quai de Bacalan, 1 Esplanade de Pontac

adult/child €20/free

🕙 10am-7pm Apr-Aug, shorter hours rest of year

2nd Floor

Sweep up the curvaceous staircase to the 2nd floor, home to the permanent exhibition. Digital companions (included in the admission fee) guide visitors around six broadly themed areas, each with plenty of interactive stations to amuse and entertain. In **Vineyards of the World** you can fly over 20 wine-making regions in 17 countries around the globe in a helicopter; **From Vine to Glass** explains wine making, grape varieties, aromas, wine families and styles; and **At the Heart of Civilisations** explores the history of wine production and trade around the world. Younger visitors will particularly enjoy smelling and sniffing their way around the Buffet of the Five Senses in the **Wine and You** themed area. In **Wine and the Imagination** film buffs (over 18 years) can watch through peep holes a series of film extracts illustrate the relationship between wine and eroticism in cinema. The **Bordeaux** themed area covers just that.

1st Floor

Temporary exhibitions, always wine-related, are held on the 1st floor. In the comfortable reading room with river view visitors can browse hundreds of wine-related reference books. Films are screened in the auditorium here.

Le Belvédère

Visits end on the 8th floor in panoramic rooftop bar **Le Belvédère** (meaning 'The Viewpoint'), an all-glass affair with a monumental 30m-long bar and a dazzling ceiling crafted from thousands of empty wine bottles. Gorge on the sensational panorama of the river, city and vineyards beyond over a complimentary glass of wine or raisin juice. Choose from red, white, rosé or sparkling, originating from 20 different countries, including Moldova, Switzerland and Georgia.

★ Top Tips

o Bordeaux Metropole City Pass holders get in free – but you must enter before noon.

o Keep a firm grip on your admission ticket – no ticket, no free glass of wine at the end of your visit.

o Guided visits depart in English (one hour, €8) several times daily, April to September.

o Get information on wine tours around Bordeaux at the ground-floor **tourist office** (Map p122, F3; www.bordeauxwinetrip.fr; 134-150 quai de Bacalan, La Cité du Vin; 10am-7pm Apr-Aug, shorter hours rest of year).

✕ Take a Break

On the 7th floor Restaurant Le 7 (p129) serves traditional French cuisine alongside mind-blowing city and river views.

For a bistro lunch or swift cheese-and-wine stop, hit the museum's ground-floor eatery **Latitude 20** (noon-7.30pm).

Top Experience 📷

See Art in a Bunker at La Base Sous-Marine

It's eyesore ugly and of sinister proportions, yet this WWII hulk of reinforced concrete by the water holds a macabre lure. Designed as a bunker to protect German u-boats from aerial attack, the submarine base proved impossible to destroy by British forces during WWII and now by Bordeaux, which uses the chilling bunker as a seriously cool cultural centre, art gallery and concert venue.

◉ MAP P122, D1

📞 05 56 11 11 50

www.facebook.com/Base sousmarinedeBordeaux

bd Alfred Daney

adult/child €5/3, free 1st Sun of month Sep-Jun

🕑 1.30-7pm Tue-Sun

History

During the Franco-Prussian War in 1870 and again at the start of WWI, when Germans threatened to advance on Paris, the French government sought refuge in Bordeaux. In June 1940, the government moved first to Tours in the Loire Valley and then to Bordeaux, although this did not save the city from heavy bombings by German troops, Nazi occupation or subsequent Allied bombings during WWII. Between 1941 and 1943, the city was a key air and submarine base for the Germans who used 6000 prisoners of war to construct reinforced-concrete submarine pens along the Atlantic Coast.

One of those five submarine bases, La Base Sous-Marine was constructed to house the Germans' 12th U-boat Flotilla. It was in use until 1944, when the Germans abandoned it in anticipation of the arrival of Allied forces in Bordeaux. Designed to be indestructible, the bunker concealed 11 submarine pens protected by a 5.6m-thick reinforced-concrete roof. An interior corridor linked the 11 pens, some of which could be emptied of water to become dry docks. An estimated 1600 German soldiers were stationed here.

Memorial

A waterfront memorial near the entrance remembers the thousands of Portuguese, Spanish and other prisoners of war who laboured on this horrific *'chantier Dantesque'* (Dantesque building site) to construct the bunker. Many perished in the process. Collapsing of hunger, illness or exhaustion, they were literally buried where they fell – in concrete.

★ Top Tips

o The base can only be visited during exhibitions.

o During exhibitions free one-hour guided tours of the submarine base depart at 5pm on Wednesday and 4pm on Saturday; reserve in advance online.

o Watch for occasional music concerts (rock, electronic, hip hop, funk etc) – the bunker is easily one of the city's edgiest live-gig venues.

✗ Take a Break

The bunker is something of an eatery wasteland: grab a gourmet picnic to go from Les Halles de Bacalan (p128) to eat by the water.

Cool off post-visit with a reviving glass of wine and tapas at Familia (p131).

Walking Tour 🥾

Urban Art Tour

In a neighbourhood with the city's Museum of Modern Art at its heart (appropriately housed in one of Chartron's signature 19th-century warehouses), it's only natural that urban art in this increasingly gentrified part of town is flourishing. Works of street art colour backstreet squares, while artist studios and experimental art projects are a dime a dozen.

Walk Facts

Start Quai des Chartrons

End Bacalan

Length 4km; one to two hours

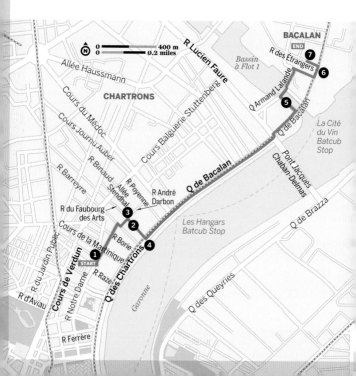

❶ Le 101

Duck into Le 101 (p135), a gallery with bright-white façade where talented graphic artist Célestin Forestier can be found working on new designs at his desk. His striking, often witty prints and posters incorporating letters or slogans make a chic souvenir to take home.

❷ Rue du Faubourg des Arts

Wedged between two 19th-century chais (wine celllars), rue du Faubourg des Arts is lined with artist workshops specialising in picture restoration, porcelain, painted furniture, leatherwork, lampshades and millinery. Most open afternoons only.

❸ The Wall

Catch an artist at work on **Le M.U.R.** (an abbreviation for 'Modular, Urban, Reactive'), or The Wall, on place Paul et Jean Paul Avisseaul. A canvas for street artists, the 35-sq-metre wall backs onto the playground of a primary school and changes monthly. Celebrity French stencil artist Jef Aérosol inaugurated it in 2014.

❹ Chartrons Skate Park

Inline skaters, boarders and BMX bikers perform jumps, spins and aerial tricks on the ramps and ledges at open-air Skate Parc des Chartrons (p128). River views are sweeping and the graffiti is a constant work-in-progress.

❺ Bassins à Flot

Meander north to industrial Bacalan where colourful tags and ephemeral wall murals brighten buildings on quai du Sénégal on the wet dock's southern edge. Some were painted in 2016 when Bassins à Flot hosted the 1st edition of Bordeaux's now-annual Shake Well street-art festival.

❻ Les Vivres de l'Art

No address evokes the experimental streak of this creative neighbourhood quite like art cooperative Les Vivres de l'Art (p125), set in an 18th-century pavilion built as a naval warehouse. Pavilion and garden are festooned with sculptures crafted from scrap metal by resident artist Jean-François Buisson and the after-dark parties thrown here are legendary.

❼ Le Garage Moderne

Hobnob with local artists at summertime-cool parties at Le Garage Moderne (p125) – yes, a garage, in a cavernous hangar with an extraordinary collection of vintage treasures and curiosities brazenly displayed between mechanic ramps.

Chartrons, Bassins à Flot & Bacalan

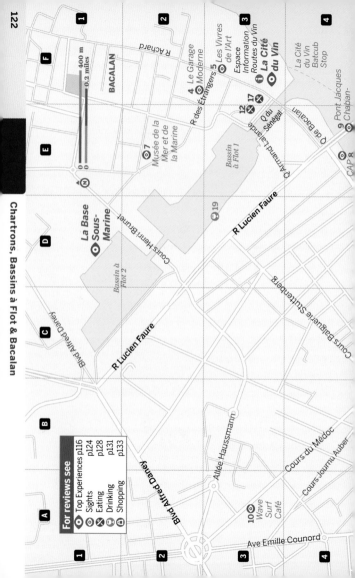

For reviews see
◎ Top Experiences p116
◎ Sights p124
✗ Eating p128
◍ Drinking p131
◩ Shopping p133

400 m
0.2 miles

BACALAN

R Achard

7 Musée de la Mer et de la Marine

La Base Sous-Marine

4 Le Garage Moderne
R des Étrangers

5 Les Vivres de l'Art
Espace Information Routes du Vin

La Cité du Vin

La Cité du Vin Batcub Stop

12

17

Q du Sénégal

Q Armand Lalande

Bassin à Flot 1

9 Pont Jacques Chaban-

Q de Bacalan

CAP R

19

Cours Henri Brunet

Bassin à Flot 2

R Lucien Faure

R Lucien Faure

Blvd Alfred Daney

Cours Balguerie Stuttenberg

Allée Haussmann

Cours du Médoc

Cours Journu Auber

10 Wave Surf Café

Ave Emille Counord

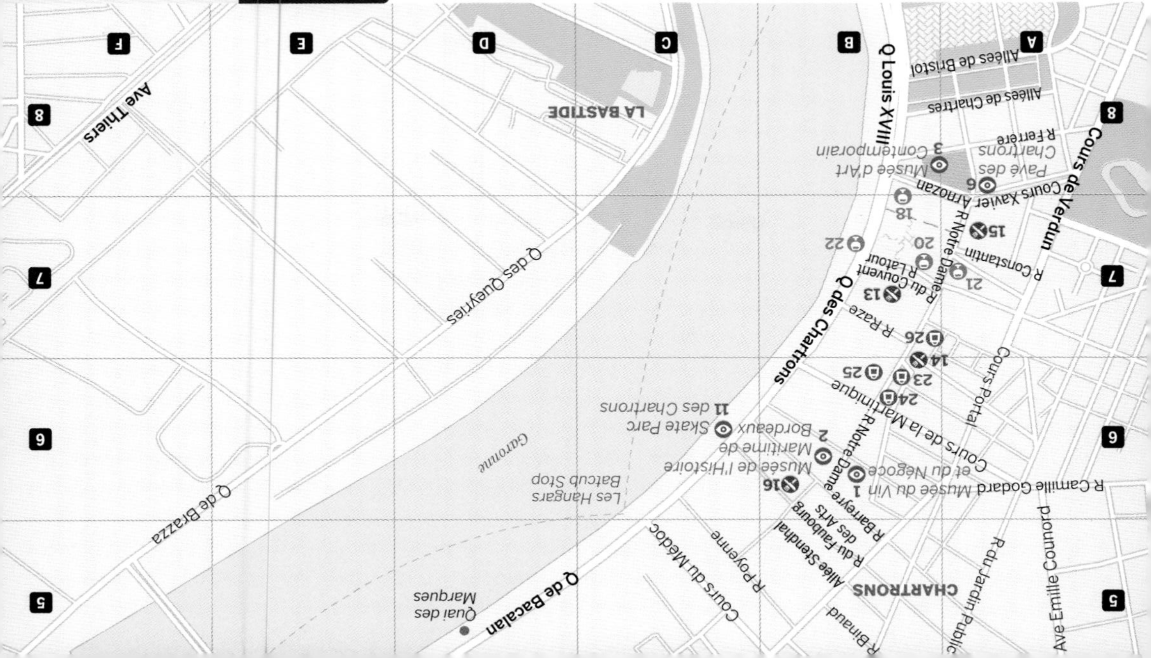

Chartrons, Bassins à Flot & Bacalan

CHARTRONS

R Binaud

Cours du Médoc

R Poyenne

R du Jardin Public

Ave Emile Counord

Allée Stendhal

R du Faubourg des Arts

R Barreyre

R Camille Godard

R Notre Dame

Cours de la Martinique

Cours Portal

Q de Bacalan

Q de Bazza

Quai des Marques

Garonne

Les Hangars
Batcub Stop

Skate Parc

Musée de l'Histoire
Maritime de
Bordeaux **2**

Q des Chartrons

Musée du Vin
et du Négoce **1**

X16

25

24

23

14 X

26

13

R Raze

P du Couvent

R Latour

20

18

22

11 des Chartrons

Q des Queyries

LA BASTIDE

Ave Thiers

Q Louis XVIII

Musée d'Art
Contemporain **3**

Cours Xavier Arnozan

Pavé des
Chartrons **6**

R Ferrère

Allées de Chartres

Allées de Bristol

R Constantin

R Notre Dame

21

15 X

Cours de Verdun

Sights

Musée du Vin et du Négoce

MUSEUM

1 MAP P122, B6

This small Wine and Trade Museum, hidden in one of the city's oldest buildings – an Irish merchant's house dating to 1720 in the ancient trading district of Chartrons – offers a fascinating insight into the historic origins of Bordeaux's wine trade and the importance of the *négociant* (merchant trader) in the 18th and 19th centuries. The vaulted cellars, 33m long, display dozens of artefacts, including hand-crafted stave oak barrels and every size of wine bottle from an Avion to a Melchior. (📞05 56 90 19 13; www.museeduvinbordeaux.com; 41 rue Borie; adult/child incl tasting €10/free; ⏱10am-6pm)

Did You Know?

The **Bourse Maritime** (former maritime stock exchange) on place Lainé was built in 1921–25 to mirror the central pavilion of place de la Bourse's **Palais de la Bourse** (stock exchange). On the façade, spot the decorative mascarons portraying the first two presidents of Bordeaux's maritime port.

Musée de l'Histoire Maritime de Bordeaux

MUSEUM

2 MAP P122, B6

Meet the shipowners, traders, explorers, navigators, poets and philosophers who contributed to the city's rich maritime history at this small, intimate museum, hidden away in a centuries-old Chartrons townhouse. Historic maps, navigational instruments and models of ships are among the fascinating exhibits that stretch from Roman to modern times. (Bordeaux Maritime History Museum; 📞05 54 51 06 39; www.museehistoiremaritime bordeaux.fr; 31 rue Borie; adult/child €5/3; ⏱10am-6pm)

Musée d'Art Contemporain

GALLERY

3 MAP P122, B8

Built in 1824 as a warehouse for French colonial produce such as coffee, cocoa, peanuts and vanilla, the cavernous Entrepôts Lainé creates a dramatic backdrop for cutting-edge modern art at Bordeaux's Museum of Contemporary Art. Highlights include works by Keith Haring and photographs of the derelict warehouse interior in the 1980s by Parisian photographer Georges Rousse.

Temporary exhibitions command a higher admission fee (adult/child €7/free). Its rooftop cafe, with a fantastic terrace, is a great spot to hang in summer. (CAPC; 📞05 56 00 81 50; www. capc-bordeaux.fr; 7 rue Ferrère; adult/

…ild €5/free, free 1st Sun of month
…p-Jun; ⏰11am-6pm Tue & Thu-Sun,
8pm Wed)

e Garage
Moderne
CULTURAL CENTRE

👁 MAP P122, F2

…trio of dedicated mechanics
…elp locals fix their own cars and
…cycles at this alternative garage
…at doubles as experimental
…ultural space in the edgy Bacalan
…istrict. Help yourself to tea or cof-
…ee, and wander around the vast
…angar packed to the rafters with
… mesmerising array of vintage
…uriosities: an old Aquitaine bus,
…inema seats, flowery crockery,
…ll sorts.

Should you bump into me-
…hanic Maud, she speaks excellent
English and will happily show you
around. Summer is the best time
to visit when the garage hosts
after-work drinks, early-evening
parties, cultural events, art exhibitions, concerts and live gigs (hip
hop, electro etc). (📞05 56 50 91 33;
www.legaragemoderne.org; 1 rue des
Étrangers; ⏰9am-5pm Mon-Sat)

Les Vivres de l'Art
GALLERY

5 👁 MAP P122, F3

Rub shoulders with bohemian
Bordeaux at this ramshackle
atelier (artist workshop) where
Jean-François Buisson, one of
several resident artists, welds
scrap metal objects into fantasti-
cal sculptures and art installa-
tions. Many of his works adorn
the shared garden, peppered with
recycled tables and chairs, a bar

…usée d'Art Contemporain

Quai des Chartrons

Over the years, this happening riverside strip has seen it all. In 1860 wealthy Dutch merchant Hilaire Renu had a twinset of identical **Flemish townhouses** constructed at Nos 28 and 29. From the quayside office here, he had a prime view of his wine barrels being loaded and unloaded onto ships destined for England and northern Europe.

Rather more sobering is the **memorial plaque** opposite 17 quai des Chartrons remembering the first slave-trade vessel that departed from the quayside in 1672. Until 1837 a further 500 voyages from Bordeaux despatched 150,000 enslaved people from Africa to the Americas.

and alternative 'dance floor'. The graceful neoclassical pavilion from 1785 was originally a military base for royal marines.

There are books to borrow in a metal 'Les Livres de l'Art' box in the garden, and the collaborative artist residency doubles as a cutting-edge venue for fringe theatre, dance and music events. DJ sets and live gigs enliven weekends. (☎05 56 10 80 94; http://lesvivresde lart.org; 4 rue Achard; ☺10am-6pm)

Pavé des Chartrons   STREET

6 ◉ MAP P122, A8

Nowhere is the immense wealth that 18th-century Bordeaux amassed from its port more explicit than on this posh avenue lined with elegant *hôtels particuliers* (mansions).

This is where wealthy wine merchants from all over Europe had their private residences. Hôtel Fenwick (1793–1800) was

built for American wine trader Joseph Fenwick who owned vines near Bordeaux. When he was appointed American consul by President George Washington in 1790, his residence on the corner of quai des Chartrons became the world's first official American consulate. (cours Xavier-Arnozan)

Musée de la Mer et de la Marine   MUSEUM

7 ◉ MAP P122, E2

This landmark new museum by the Basins à Flot comprises three floors of exhibition space devoted to almost everything there is to know about Bordeaux's maritime world, including its history, science, culture and traditions.

Themes include the history of navigation and discovery, naval battles, the scientific conquest of the Atlantic and the fascinating world of oceanography. The building – a striking work of contempo-

ry architecture designed to look
e an ocean liner – was designed
local Bordeaux architect Olivier
ochet.

In front of the main entrance,
e shimmering 7m-tall shark
rung up like a hunting trophy was
culpted by French artist Philippe
asqua in 2017. It evokes the
stimated 100 million sharks killed
orldwide by humans each year,
sking the species' eventual exter-
ination. (www.museedelamerbor
eaux.fr; 89 rue des Étrangers)

AP Sciences MUSEUM

◉ MAP P122, E4

n imposing concrete hangar on
ne riverfront is the venue for this
utting-edge science museum,
ost to various temporary exhibi-
ons focusing on anything from
obotics or digital meditation to
enewable energy, the stars, time
r light.

Exhibitions are always interac-
ve and cast a new spin on tradi-
onal boundaries of museology.

Themed activity workshops for
ids include astronomy, film-
naking, green chemistry, photo-
raphy and culinary experiments
n the Labo Miam; reserve in
dvance online. (📞 05 56 01 07 07;
ww.cap-sciences.net; quai de Bacalan,
angar 20; admission varies; ⏲2-6pm
ue-Thu, to 9pm Fri, to 7pm Sat & Sun)

Pont Jacques Chaban-Delmas BRIDGE

9 ◉ MAP P122, E4

Europe's highest lift bridge crosses
the River Garonne with grace and
aplomb near the entrance to the
Bassins à Flot.

At night, its four distinctive
pylons towering 77m tall are illumi-
nated blue at high tide and green
at low tide.

Unveiled in 2013, the bridge is
named after Jacques Chaban-
Delmas, prime minister under
French president Georges Pom-
pidou (1969–72) and mayor of
Bordeaux for a remarkable eight
terms or 48 years (1947–95).

Wave Surf Café SURFING

10 ◉ MAP P122, A3

Try your hand at *glisse urbain*
(aka urban surfing) at this funky
surfing cafe, complete with indoor
artificial wave. Introductory surfing and body-surfing sessions last

Sunday Morning Quayside

The quays along the Garonne
buzz by day with joggers,
bladers and afternoon
flâneurs (strollers), but it is
during the vibrant Sunday
morning food market on quai
des Chartrons that a hypnotic
bazaar of colour, aroma and
noise unfolds.

55 minutes and you can rent a shorty wetsuit for €2. Reserve in advance. (☎09 83 29 67 74; www.wave-surf-cafe.fr; 174 cours du Médoc; €24; ☺2-9pm Mon, 10am-9pm Tue-Sun)

Skate Parc des Chartrons

SPORTS

11 ◉ MAP P122, C6

Mingle with local skateboarders, roller-bladers and BMX tricksters at Bordeaux's open-air skate park.

It's set in an enviable location next to the river on the waterfront. (quai des Chartrons; ☺9am-10pm)

Eating

Les Halles de Bacalan

FOOD HALL

12 ✖ MAP P122, E3

At home in a waterfront hangar opposite La Cité du Vin, this gleaming state-of-the-art market hall is a fantastic spot to grab a quick gourmet bite. Some 20 upmarket stalls cooking up everything from fish, burgers and meat to oysters, poultry, Italian products and cheese serve a daily menu. Seating is at bar stools or outside overlooking the wet docks. (☎05 56 80 63 65; www.facebook.com/hallesdebacalan; 149 quai de Bacalan; ☺8am-2.30pm 5.30-8.30pm Tue & Wed, to 10pm Thu Fri, 8am-2am Sat, 8am-5pm Sun)

Skate Parc des Chartrons

e 7 Restaurant   FRENCH €€

dine with a bird's-eye view of
e industrial port, river and city
eyond (see La Cité du Vin ⊙ Map p122, F3),
ead up to this dazzling mirage
f glass, steel and gold on the
th floor of La Cité du Vin (p116).
terior design is overwhelmingly
ontemporary, cuisine is tradi-
onal French (Burgundy snails,
aviar, steaks) with an occasional
reative flourish and the extensive
ine list is iPad-searchable. (📞05
4 31 05 40; www.le7restaurant.com;
84-150 quai de Bacalan, La Cité du Vin;
/3-course menu lunch €25/32, din-
er €65, mains €21-36; ⏰noon-3pm &
10.30pm, cafe 10am-10pm)

u Couvent   MEDITERRANEAN €

🍴 MAP P122, B7

xposed stone walls, vintage
replace and windowsills dotted
ith flower pots add instant charm
this backstreet address run by
e talented Marine. Sinful dishes
n the menu – 'les péchés' means
ins' in French – include tempta-
ons such as artichoke carpaccio
a truffle-laced dressing, chicken
nd peanut donuts and mini burg-
rs. Sunday brunch is a supremely
vial, stylish affair. Reserve online.
📞07 83 16 84 87; www.aucouvent.
m; 23 rue du Couvent; 2-/3-course
nch menu €15/19, brunch €29, mains
17; ⏰11.30am-3pm Tue, 11.30am-
om & 6.30pm-1am Wed-Sat, 11am-
30pm Sun)

Chartrons Wine Fest

One of the most festive
moments to rub shoulders
with the soul of this 'hood
is during its **Fête du Vin
Nouveau et de la Brocante**,
a two-day street festival in
October thrown to celebrate
the first post-harvest wine.
The *vin nouveau* (new wine)
is solemnly blessed in church
before the real party breaks
out on rue Notre Dame and
surrounding streets: think
drinking, dancing, street food
and dozens of stalls selling
antiques and secondhand
jumble.

Bocca a bocca   ITALIAN €€

Locals can't get enough of this
candlelit trattoria with summer
terrace on Chartron's main street
(see 14 🍴 Map p122, B6). Meal-size
salads bursting with grilled au-
bergines, mozzarella, San Daniele
cured meat and other typical Italian products vie for attention with
cold-meat platters and tempting
mains like gorgonzola-laced polen-
ta with pancetta and baby spinach
leaves or a Bocca burger stuffed
with creamy burrata cheese and
grilled veg. (📞05 57 83 69 66; www.
epicerielabocca.com; 75 rue Notre
Dame; mains €10-20; ⏰noon-2.30pm
& 7.15-10.15pm Tue-Sat)

Bordeaux Wine

Bordeaux's rich swathe of vineyards cover 120,000 hectares on both sides of the River Garonne, prompting the eternal debate over which bank – Rive Gauche (Left Bank) and Rive Droite (Right Bank) – is best. Robust and generous, the vines are tended by 6300 *vignerons* (winemakers) who produce up to 5.7 million hectolitres of red, white, rosé and sparkling wines each year using various grape varieties. Every second, 21 bottles of Bordeaux wine are sold around world.

Appellations

The entire Bordeaux region is divided into 65 appellations (production areas whose soil and microclimate impart distinctive characteristics to the wine produced there). Each geographic subregion produces at least two or three different appellations – some produce up to a dozen.

Unusually for a wine-growing region, almost all Bordeaux wines have earned the right to include the abbreviation AOC (Appellation d'Origine Contrôlée) on their labels. A stamp of quality, this indicates that the bottle's contents have been grown, fermented and aged according to strict regulations that govern a mind-boggling variety of viticultural matters such as the number of vines permitted per hectare, acceptable pruning methods or harvesting technique.

Classifications

It was at the 1855 Universal Exhibition in Paris, thrown to show off France's prowess to the world, that Napoleon III asked wine merchants from Bordeaux to come up with a classification – effectively quality ranking – for the wine they were exhibiting to help visitors sort the wheat from the chaff. This was the first time wine had been so blatantly ranked and the resultant list produced by this 1855 Bordeaux Classification remains a Holy Grail in the wine world.

Further classifications have been added, but it's the 60 chateaux from the Médoc and Graves on the original list that remain the most venerated. The top five chateaux classified as *premier cru* ('first growth') – Château Mouton Rothschild, Château Latour and Château Lafite-Rothschild (all AOC Pauillac), Château Margaux (AOC Margaux) and in Graves, Château Haut-Brion (AOC Pessac-Léognan) – are the gods of Bordeaux winemakers, with price tags to match.

a Copa Rota

MEXICAN €

⊗ MAP P122, B6

his tiny but colourful *taquería* eaves with students feasting n its excellent-value, seriously uthentic tacos, quesadillas and ther Mexican dishes prepared by e gregarious Claudia Flores. Mar- aritas and other boozy tequila- ased cocktails are the perfect ccompaniment. Reservations es- ential; no credit cards. (📞06 37 77 4 58; www.facebook.com/lacoparota; 7 rue Notre Dame; tacos & quesadillas 3-6, plat du jour €10; ⊗12.30-3pm & 30-10pm)

harli & Tom

HEALTH FOOD €

⊗ MAP P122, A7

lade-to-measure salads are the peciality of this inspired eatery cross the street from the Temple e Chartrons. Pick from dozens f different green leaves, grains, eeds, veg and toppings to com- ose your own *salade sur mesure*, ced with one of six different ressings. Homemade soups and avoury tarts beef up the healthy nenu. Eat in or take away. (📞05 5 48 73 84; www.charli-tom.fr; 11 rue otre Dame; salads €6-11; ⊗11am- 30pm Mon-Fri)

AC

CAFE €

⊗ MAP P122, B6

obnob with students over a Chicken Révolution' bagel, spiced eef samosas or Mexican salad ith red beans and fried chorizo

at this cafe-bar in the reinvented wine cellars of 19th-century wine merchant Alfred de Luze. Outside seating is beneath a wonderful steel-and-glass roof linking the two huge hangar-like *chais* (cellars) to form a gallery. (Zone d'Activité Culinaire; 📞09 54 80 53 03; www. zac-restaurant-chartrons.fr; 89 quai des Chartrons; mains €8-10; ⊗7am- 5.30pm Mon-Fri, 8am-3pm Sat; 📶)

Familia

BISTRO €€

17 ⊗ MAP P122, F3

Named after the cinema that animated the 'hood in the 1920s, Familia is a large, light-flooded eatery across the street from Bordeaux's La Cité du Vin. Snack on casual, tapas-style bites served in small glass conserve jars at Le Comptoir ('The Counter') and a meatier market cuisine at meal times in its Brasserie. (Brasserie des Halles; 📞05 56 07 36 15; www.familia- brasserie.fr; Esplanade de Pontac; tapas €6-10, mains €12-40; ⊗bras- serie noon-midnight, Le Comptoir 11am-2am, cafe 9am-2am Mon-Sat, to 8pm Sun; 📶♿)

Drinking

Symbiose

COCKTAIL BAR

18 🚇 MAP P122, B7

There is something inviting about this clandestine address with a soft green façade across from the river on the fringe of the Chartrons district. This is the

Bargain Shopping

Scoop up big-name fashion brands at a snip of the full price in the many outlet stores inside **Quai des Marques** (Map p122, D5; www.quaides marques.com/bordeaux; quai des Chartrons; ⏰10am-7pm Tue-Sun), a riverside shopping mall comprising four huge, waterfront hangars once used to store wine but now sparkling with the latest cutting-edge fashion. Inside are some 30 outlet stores, including dozens of big-names such as Hugo Boss, Reebok and Swiss chocolate-maker Lindt.

secret speakeasy that introduced good cocktails with gastronomic food pairings to Bordeaux. The chef uses locally sourced artisan products, and cocktails rekindle old-fashioned recipes packed with homemade syrups and 'forgotten', exotic or unusual ingredients. (Old-fashioned Stories; 📞05 56 23 67 15; www.facebook.com/symbiosebordeaux; 4 quai des Chartrons; ⏰noon-2.30pm Mon, noon-2.30pm & 6.30pm-2am Tue-Fri, 6.30pm-2am Sat)

I.Boat CLUB

19 📍 MAP P122, D3

Hip hop, rock, indie pop, psyche blues rock, punk and hardcore are among the varied sounds that blast out of this fun nightclub and concert venue, on a decommissioned ferry moored in the increasingly trendy, industrial Bassins à Flot district in the north of the city. Live music starts at 7pm, with DJ sets kicking in on the club dance floor from 11.30pm. (📞05 56 10 48 37; www.iboat.eu; quai Armand Lalande, Bassins à Flot 1; ⏰7.30pm-6am)

Le Zytho CRAFT BEER

20 📍 MAP P122, B7

Craft-beer lovers will be in heaven in this cavernous beer bar, an urban-smart place to kick back beneath gold-stone vaults over one of 100 bottled beers or 18 on tap. Excellent tapas dishes accompany drinks – order the perfect four-tapas, four-beer food pairing to avoid agonising over your options. Kudos for the playful rocking chairs and free photomat (snaps are sent later by email). (📞09 83 23 03 03; http://lezytho.fr; 28 rue Latour; ⏰5.30pm-midnight Tue & Wed, 5.30pm-1am Thu-Sat)

La Pelle Café COFFEE

21 📍 MAP P122, A7

With exposed gold-stone walls and a soothing, slate-blue colour palette, this contemporary coffee shop in Bordeaux's vintage wine-merchant district is a relaxed place to sit back and chill over a serious espresso made from carefully selected, home-

asted green beans. Filter coffee
barista Théo's first love, but
verything is good here, includ-
g the fantastically handsome
eetroot latte with a green-tea-
nd-white-chocolate cookie on
e side. (☑05 56 81 69 24; www.
bellecafe.com; 29 rue Notre Dame;
9am-6pm Tue, Wed & Fri, to 10pm
u, 10am-6pm Sat & Sun)

aïa Café CAFE

☑ 🟢 MAP P122, B7

he living is easy at this chic
aterfront address, a hybrid cafe-
ar serving drinks and tapas-style
shes, grilled fish *à la plancha* and
ther light Mediterranean dishes
a good-looking crowd. Giant
otted palms inject an instant

beach feel to the place and river
views are naturally first-class.
(☑05 56 00 45 35; www.facebook.
com/ibaia.cafe; opp quai des Chartrons
24; ⏱10am-6pm Sun & Mon, to 2am
Tue-Sat)

Shopping

Do You Speak
Français? CONCEPT STORE

23 🔒 MAP P122, B6

Gaëlle and Maxime are the
creative duo behind this inspiring
concept store stocking fashionable tote bags, t-shirts, fashion
accessories and homewares. The
boutique is easy to spot – look for
the wrought-iron balcony painted
candyfloss-pink above the ground

uai des Marques

Wine Sub-Regions of Bordeaux

Bordeaux vineyards fall into a handful of sub-regions.

Graves & Sauternes

Bordeaux's beautiful viticulture adventure began in Graves, immediately south of Bordeaux city on the Garonne's Left Bank, where the very first vine stock was planted in the year 1 CE. One of Bordeaux's best known whites, Pessac-Léognan, is produced here, as are its finest world-famous *vins liquoreux* (sweet wines): the slow, labour-intensive grape harvest for Sauternes and Barsac wines is performed exclusively by hand in October and November and grapes are sorted thrice to ensure world-class quality; 2014 is an outstanding vintage.

Entre-deux-Mers

On the opposite side of the Garonne, southeast of Bordeaux city, is the 'Between the Tides' wine-producing area, named after its unique 'sandwich' location between the Garonne and Dordogne rivers. More than 50% of Bordeaux wine, notably whites, grow here.

Le Libournais

Planted on both banks of a trio of rivers (the Dordogne, Dronne and Isle) east of Bordeaux city, this interesting region includes hot-shot names such as Pomerol, Fronsac and St-Émilion (p112).

Blaye & Bourg

Moving north, still on the right bank of the Dordogne River and also the Gironde Estuary into which the river spills en route to the Atlantic, this wine-growing sub-region produces red and dry whites from a blend of the most staunchly traditional Bordeaux grape varieties (Merlot, Cabernet Sauvignon and Sauvignon). Its notably hilly vineyards trap bags of sun.

Médoc

Across the water, on the Left Bank of the Garonne and Gironde Estuary immediately northwest of Bordeaux city, is the celebrated Médoc – a vast, exclusive red-wine producing zone with an oceanic climate and wine hub and port town, Pauillac, at its heart. A relatively 'young' wine-growing area in Bordelaise speak, vines were only planted here in the 18th century.

...oor shop front. (☎ 06 24 99 64 12;
www.facebook.com/doyouspeakfran
ais; 93 rue Notre Dame; ⓘ 11am-7pm
ue-Sat)

...e 101 ART

...4 🔒 MAP P122, B6

...he playful and oftentimes clever
...rints and posters incorporat-
...g letters and words by graphic
...esigner Célestin Forestier make
... beautiful souvenir-with-a-
...ifference to take home. (☎ 05 57
...2 99 64; www.101-lesite.com; 101 rue
...otre Dame; ⓘ 9am-7pm Mon-Sat)

...'Atelier HOMEWARES

...5 🔒 MAP P122, B6

...rowse this attractive artisan-
...lass workshop and boutique for

uniquely crafted mirrors, jewellery
and *objets deco* (decorative
objects) for the home. (☎ 09 80 99
53 69; www.latelierbordeaux.com; 88
rue Notre Dame; ⓘ 10am-12.30pm &
2-7pm Tue-Sat)

Village Notre Dame ANTIQUES

26 🔒 MAP P122, B7

Browse stall after stall, laden with
17th- to 20th-century furniture
and ornaments, tapestries and
trinkets, paintings, household
items and silverware at this vast
antiques gallery, at home in a
former printing house. Be it a
portrait of Napoleon III, an antique
globe from 1857 or a silver teapot
from the 19th century, you'll find it
here. (61-67 rue Notre Dame; ⓘ 10am-
12.30pm & 2-7pm)

The Médoc

Northwest of Bordeaux, along the western shore of the Gironde Estuary – formed by the confluence of the Garonne and Dordogne Rivers – lie some of Bordeaux's most celebrated vineyards. Eight appellations come out of the Médoc region, some of the finest wine territory in the world bolstered by mythical powerhouses like Mouton Rothschild, Latour and Lafite Rothschild.

Getting There

🚗 The lack of public transport to most of the chateaux means this area is best explored with your own car. Count an hour's drive from downtown Bordeaux or 50 minutes from the airport.

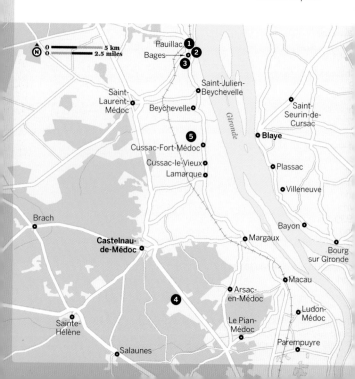

❶ Pauillac

On the banks of the muddy Gironde, the port town of Pauillac (population 1300), 47km north of Bordeaux, is at the heart of the vine country. It is surrounded by the distinguished Haut-Médoc, Margaux and St-Julien appellations and extraordinary chateaux pepper its vine-stitched landscape, from the world-famous Château Ducru-Braucaillou on its southeast fringe to Château Margaux. The Pauillac vine appellation encompasses 18 *crus classés,* including the world-renowned Mouton Rothschild, Latour and Lafite Rothschild.

❷ Château Lynch-Bages

Château Lynch-Bages (☏05 56 73 19 31; www.jmcazes.com/en/chateau-lynch-bages; Craste des Jardins, Pauillac; 1hr visit with tasting €9, 2½hr tastings €75; ⏲9.30am-1pm & 2.30-6pm), gracefully set in the wealthy hamlet of Bages, 2km southwest of Pauillac, is one of the best-known Médoc wineries – due in no small part to the extraordinary energy, passion and charisma of the Cazes family who have owned the estate since 1939. It is one of the region's oldest, and its wine was among the 18 prestigious Cinquièmes Crus classified in 1855 (p130). Each year an artist is invited to the chateau to create a work of art for it.

❸ Café Lavinal

The menu at this enchanting, 1930s-styled village **bistro** (☏05 57 75 00 09; www.jmcazes.com/en/cafe-lavinal; place Desquet, Bages; menus €28-38, mains €27-29; ⏲8am-2pm & 7.30-9pm; ❄🐾) on the village square in Bages is overseen by Michelin-starred chef Julien Lefebvre from neighbouring Château Cordeillan-Bages. With 120 wines on the *carte de vin,* a brilliant dining experience is guaranteed.

❹ La Winery

Don't miss Philippe Raoux's vast glass-and-steel wine centre, **La Winery** (☏05 56 39 04 90; www.winery.fr; rte du Verdon, Rond-point des Vendangeurs, Arsac-en-Médoc; ⏲10.30am-7.30pm Tue-Sun, boutique 10am-8pm Jun-Sep, to 7.30pm Oct-May), which mounts concerts and contemporary-art exhibits alongside various fee-based tastings, including innovative tastings that determine your *signe œnologique* ('wine sign'), costing €25 (11am and 4pm daily; booking required). Its boutique stocks more than 1000 different wines.

❺ Château Lanessan

Hour-long guided tours at **Château Lanessan** (☏05 56 58 94 80; www.lanessan.com; Cussac-Fort-Medoc; adult/child €15/free; ⏲10am-noon & 2-6pm by advance reservation) take in the neoclassical chateau, its English-style gardens, 19th-century greenhouse, wine cellars, the stables, pine-panelled tack room and a horse museum with several 19th-century horse-drawn carriages. Tours end with wine tasting. Reserve at least one day in advance.

Worth a Trip 📲

Bassin d'Arcachon

When the urban Bordelais feel the need for some serious fresh air and seaside frolics, they head 65km southwest to the tranquil, triangular Bay of Arcachon (Bassin d'Arcachon), at the lower edge of the Atlantic Coast. With generous swathes of sheltered, golden-sand beaches, a thriving oyster culture and cycling paths galore, there is no finer spot to re-energise urban souls - or simply indulge in a delightful day out.

Getting There

🚆🚌 Frequent trains link Bordeaux's Gare St-Jean with Arcachon train station (€11.50, one hour), from where local Baia bus line 1 (www.bus-baia.fr) continues to the Dune du Pilat (€1, 30 minutes, at least hourly).

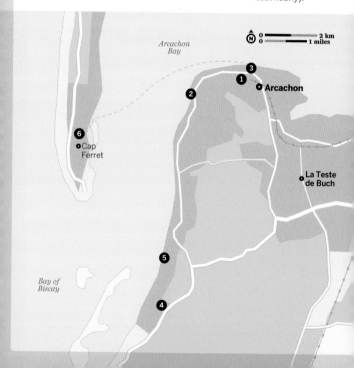

Arcachon

long-time oyster-harvesting area on the southern side of the bay, this elegant seaside town lured bourgeois Bordelaise at the end of the 19th century. Its four little quarters are romantically named for each of the seasons, with villas that evoke the town's golden past amid a scattering of 1950s architecture.

2 Plage d'Arcachon

Hit the beach! In Arcachon's delightful Ville d'Été (Summer Quarter), deep sandy Plage d'Arcachon is flanked by two piers. Lively Jetée Thiers is at the western end, from where boats yo-yo across the water to Cap Ferret. The eastern pier, Jetée d'Eyrac, is lauded over by an old-fashioned carousel, a vintage Big Wheel and the town's turreted casino.

3 Coastal Bike Ride

By the beachfront, grab a bike from **Dingo Vélos** (☑05 56 83 44 09; www.dingovelos.com; 1 rue Grenier; 4hr/1 day €10/13) and peddle 8km south along silky smooth cycling paths skimming the coast and through scented pine forests to the eye-popping Dune du Pilat.

4 Dune du Pilat

Scramble up Europe's largest sand dune with the aid of a wooden staircase (Easter to mid-Nov) or bare-footed on the shifting sand – ice cold in winter, as hot as burning coals in summer – and admire the mind-blowing view from the top. This colossal sand dune, 4km from the tiny seaside resort town of Pyla-sur-Mer, stretches from the mouth of the Bassin d'Arcachon southwards for 2.7km. It's growing eastwards 1.5m a year and has already swallowed trees, a road junction and even a hotel, so local lore claims.

5 Lunch with View

Lap up coastal glamour at 1930s hunting lodge-turned-design-sharp hotel-restaurant, **La Co(o)rniche** (☑05 56 22 72 11; www.lacoorniche-pyla.com; 46 av Louis Gaume; 2-/3-course lunch menu €58/63, seafood platters €40-85). Perfectly placed for a meal or tapas-fuelled drink after a sandy hike on the dune, this sensational seaside address cooks up modern French cuisine and unforgettable dune views. Snag a table by the infinity pool or, should you prefer a cheaper or lighter dine, flop with a cocktail and seafood tapas in a cushioned canapé in the bar.

6 Cap Ferret

Back in Arcachon, hop aboard a boat (adult/child €7/5, 30 minutes, at least hourly) to the tiny and deliciously oyster-rich village of Cap Ferret, hidden in a canopy of pine trees on the tip of the Cap Ferret peninsula. Pedalling between oyster shacks and out to the lighthouse on the cape's eastern shore are deliciously old-fashioned highlights of any visit here.

Survival Guide

Bordeaux tram s-fa/shutterstock ©

Before You Go

Book Your Stay

o Book ahead in season (spring to early autumn), especially for weekend stays.

o Dead-central Saint-Pierre, Saint-Paul and Quinconces offer a wide range of sleeping options for all budgets – all within walking distance of Bordeaux's key sights, nightlife venues, vibrant dining scene and mainstream shopping strips.

o Hotels in pedestrian Saint-Pierre are only accessibly on foot or accessible by car at limited times. Cheaper hotels, with rooms overlooking major pedestrian thoroughfares in Saint-Pierre's medieval heart, can be noisy.

o If it's hardcore Bordelais charm and tasty dining you're seeking, consider a midrange B&B or historic townhouse hotel in village-like Chartrons. The neighbourhood requires a short walk or tram ride to get to and

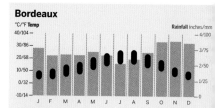

Bordeaux
°C/°F Temp   Rainfall inches/mm

When to Go

o **Winter** (Dec–Feb) Mild winter temperatures, with a real chill at night. Tourists are few, making it an ideal time to explore the city *sans* the crowds.

o **Spring** (Mar–May) Days are warm, flowers blossom, markets burst with produce and cafe life is al fresco.

o **Summer** (Jun–Aug) It's sizzling hot in the city now, with a packed lineup of festivals, outdoor concerts and other cultural events.

o **Autumn** (Sep-Nov) Leaves blush crimson and gold, and sun-filled grapes are harvested during the *vendange* (grape harvest).

from, although La Cité du Vin and the riverfront are right next door.

Useful Websites

Bordeaux Tourisme (www.bordeaux-tourism.com) Comprehensive accommodation listings (hotels, serviced apartments, B&Bs, hostels etc) from the tourist office.

Bordeaux Apartments (https://bordeauxapartments.fr) Stylish, self-catering apartments in central Bordeaux.

Lonely Planet (lonelyplanet.com/hotels) Recommendations on where to stay.

Best Budget

Hôtel Notre Dame (https://hotelbordeaux chartrons.com) Vintage rooms in the 'village' heart of Chartrons.

Hôtel de la Presse (www.hoteldelapresse.com) Excellent value design hotel on a busy shopping street.

Hôtel du Théâtre (www.hotel-du-theatre.com) Small, down-to-

earth spot near place
de la Comédie.

Auberge de Jeunesse
(www.auberge-jeu
nesse-bordeaux.com)
For many years, the
city's only hostel.

Best Midrange

**Ecolodge des
Chartrons** (www.
ecolodgedeschartrons.
com) Old-world charm-
ing, eco-conscious B&B
in Chartrons.

Maison Fredon (www.
latupina.com/maison
-d-hotes-fredon-bord
eaux) Bourgeois guest-
house on a foodie street
in St-Michel.

Mama Shelter (www.
mamashelter.com/en/
bordeaux) Sharp snap-
py, Philippe Starck–digs
in a 1927 tower block.

Hôtel La Cour Carrée
(www.lacourcarree.
com) Contemporary
decor and gold-stone
walls meet in a 19th-
century townhouse with
peaceful courtyard in
upmarket Saint-Seurin.

**Hôtel Bordeaux
Clemenceau** (http://
en.hotel-bordeaux
-clemenceau.com)
Three-star family fa-
vourite amongst shops
on a busy street near
the Triangle d'Or.

Best Top End

**Grand Hôtel de
Bordeaux** (https://
bordeaux.intercon
tinental.com) The
ultimate historic and
luxurious choice with
Michelin-starred dining
and sensational rooftop
'beach' bar.

Chez Dupont (www.
chez-dupont.com)
Contemporary, design-
driven B&B in Bor-
deaux's wine-merchant
district.

L'Hôtel Particulier
(www.lhotel-particuli
er.com) Thoughtfully
designed rooms and
self-catering apart-
ments in a historic
mansion right by the
cathedral.

Hôtel de Sèze (www.
hotel-de-seze.com)
Chic spa-hotel by the
upmarket Triangle d'Or.

Le Boutique Hôtel
(https://hotelbordeaux
centre.com) Four-star
luxury in a beauti-
ful 18th-century
hôtel particulier (private
mansion) in chic Saint-
Seurin.

Yndō Hôtel (https://
yndohotelbordeaux.
fr) Uber-chic hotel
with stunning
contemporary-art
collection.

Best B&Bs

Maison Fredon (www.
latupina.com/maison
-d-hotes-fredon-bord
eaux) Five-room
B&B in a bourgeois
townhouse near Saint-
Michel.

Chez Dupont (www.
chez-dupont.com) Ten
chic, vintage-dressed
rooms in village-like
Chartrons.

**Ecolodge des
Chartrons** (www.
ecolodgedeschartrons.
com) Eco-friendly
rooms and bags of
old-world charm in
Chartrons.

L'Hôtel Particulier
(www.lhotel-particulier.
com) Luxurious pe-
riod rooms near the
cathedral.

**Les Chambres au
Coeur de Bordeaux**
(www.aucoeurde
bordeaux.fr) Homey,
midrange choice on
the fringe of Saint-
Pierre.

Best Hôtels
Particuliers

Hôtel La Cour Carrée
(www.lacourcarree.
com) Unpretentious,
midrange address with
a peaceful courtyard in
chic Saint-Seurin.

Hôtel Continental

(http://en.hotel-le-continental.com) Check into an 18th-century *hôtel particulier* which was known as Hôtel du Coq 'Or in 1912.

Yndō Hôtel (https://yndohotelbordeaux.fr)

Compelling contemporary art marries perfectly with this luxury boutique hotel's historic setting.

Le Boutique Hôtel

(https://hotelbordeauxcentre.com) Four-star luxury in a beautiful Saint-Seurin mansion from the 18th century.

Best Design Hotels

Seeko'o Hôtel

(https://seekoo-hotel.com) Dazzling, all-white and curvaceous, contemporary design near La Cité du Vin.

Mama Shelter (www.mamashelter.com/en/bordeaux)

Bright white walls broken with bursts of colour are trademarks of this Philippe Starck art work.

Yndō Hôtel (https://yndohotelbordeaux.fr)

Outstanding contemporary art by Bordelais

artists and chic designer furnishings in a historic townhouse.

Hôtel de Sèze (www.hotel-de-seze.com)

Four-star spa-hotel named after a St-Émilion count.

Hôtel de la Presse

(www.hoteldelapresse.com) Cheap 'n' cheerful hotel in Saint-Pierre with a giant dog in the breakfast room and print-themed rooms.

Arriving in Bordeaux

Aéroport de Bordeaux

Aéroport de Bordeaux (Bordeaux Airport;

BOD; ✈ Information 05 56 34 50 50; www.bordeaux.aeroport.fr; Mérignac), also known as Bordeaux-Mérignac, is 10km west of the city centre in the suburb of Mérignac. Domestic and increasing numbers of international flights to/from many western European and North African destinations use one of three neighbouring terminals here. Low-

cost airlines – including Easyjet, FlyBe and Hop! – use the basic Billi Terminal; others use adjoining A or B.

Bus

Urban bus line 1+, operated by public-transport company TBM (www.infotbm.com), links the airport with place Gambetta, place de la Victoire and the Gare St-Jean train station in town. At the airport, buy tickets (€1.70) from the ticket dispenser next to the bus stop, in front of Terminal B, or directly from the driver. Buses run every 10 minutes or so between 6am to 11pm and the journey time is 40 minutes (longer at rush hour).

The notably pricier, not swifter 30'Direct shuttle bus (http://keolis-aquitaine.com; €8, 30 to 40 minutes, longer in rush hour) has free wi-fi onboard and also links Terminal B with Gare St-Jean. Buses depart roughly every 30 to 45 minutes between 7.40am (later at weekends) and 8.30pm. Buy tickets online or from the driver.

Taxi

A taxi between the city centre and airport costs around €50.

Car & Motorcycle

Major car-rental companies have offices inside the main airport terminal.

Gare St-Jean

Bordeaux is one of France's major rail-transit points, served since July 2017 by the LGV (ligne à grand vitesse) that sees high-speed TGV trains to/from Paris cruising between Bordeaux and Tours in the Loire Valley at speeds of 320km/h. This puts Bordeaux just six hours from London by Eurostar (www.eurostar.com), with a change of train in Paris.

Bordeaux train station, **Gare St-Jean** (Cours de la Marne), retains much of its original grandeur from 1855. A major spruce-up in 2017 saw the construction of Hall 3, a contemporary all-glass building with shops and cafes to compliment the station's other two halls.

Bus & Tram

From in front of the train station, catch bus line 1 to place de la Victoire or tram line C north along the river to public transport hub Esplanade des Quinconces (€1.70).

Getting Around

Bus & Tram

o Urban buses and trams are run by TBM (www.infotbm.com) between 5am and 1am. Get timetable information and tickets from its **Espace des Quinconces** (Map p54, D2; ☏05 57 57 88 88; www.infotbm.com; Esplanade des Quinconces; ☉7am-7pm Mon-Fri, 9am-7pm Sat) information office, the main bus and tram hub.

o Tram line C links the latter with the train station via the riverside; tram B cruises north along the river to Bassins à Flot and La Cité du Vin.

o Rechargeable, contactless tickets (single journey €1.70) are sold onboard buses, and from machines at tram stops (validate your ticket onboard). You can also buy a carnet (book) of 10 tickets (€13.20) or a one-day ticket covering unlimited travel (€4.70).

Bicycle

o Public bike-sharing scheme V³ (www.vcub.fr), run by local public transport company TBM, has 1800 banana-yellow bicycles available for use at bike stations all over the city.

o Pay €1.70 to access a bike for 24 hours, plus €2 per hour after the first 30 minutes (free) is up; you'll need to initially register online or with your credit card at a V³ station.

Boat

o B³ (www.infotbm.com) boats shuttle between quai des Maréchal Lyautey (by Palais de la Bourse), quai de Bacalan (by Quai des Marques shopping mall and La Cité du Vin) and quay des Queyries on the right bank (near Magasin Général).

◦ Tickets cost €2 and are sold on board.

Car & Motorcycle

◦ City parking is pricey and hard to find. Look for free spaces in the side streets north of the Musée d'Art Contemporain and west of Jardin Public.

◦ Yugo (www.getyugo. com/bordeaux) is an electric-scooter sharing scheme, accessed via an app that allows users to geolocate one of 50 free-floating, peppermint-green scooters and reserve it for 15 minutes – the time to get to the located spot. Pay €0.22 per minute.

Taxi

◦ To order call 05 56 29 10 25, or pick one up on place de la Victoire.

Essential Information

Accessible Travel

◦ Bordeaux presents evident challenges – cobblestones, cafe-lined streets that are a nightmare to navigate

in a wheelchair (*fauteuil roulant*), a lack of kerb ramps, older public facilities and many budget hotels without lifts – but efforts are being made to improve the situation and with careful planning, a hassle-free accessible stay is possible.

◦ Download Lonely Planet's free Accessible Travel guides from http://lptravel.to/AccessibleTravel.

Business Hours

Banks 9am–noon and 2pm–5pm Monday to Friday or Tuesday to Saturday.

Bars 7pm–1am.

Cafes 7am–11pm.

Clubs 10pm–3am, 4am or 5am Thursday to Saturday.

Restaurants Noon–2.30pm and 7pm–11pm six days a week; most typically closed Monday or Tuesday.

Shops 10am–noon and 2pm–7pm Monday to Saturday.

Discount Cards

Bordeaux Métropole City Pass (www.bordeauxcitypass.

com; 24/48/72 hours €29/39/46) covers admission to 20 museums and monuments. It also includes a free guided tour and unlimited use of public buses, trams and boats. Buy it online or at the **tourist office** (Map p54; ☎ 05 56 00 66 00; www.bordeaux-tourisme.com; 12 cours du 30 Juillet; ⏰ 9am-6.30pm Mon-Sat, to 5pm Sun).

Electricity

Type E
230V/50Hz

Emergency & Important Numbers

To dial a Bordeaux phone number from another country, dial

our international
ccess code, France's
ountry code and then
he local telephone
umber minus the
nitial '0'. France has no
rea codes, meaning
ou simply dial the
0-digit Bordeaux
umber from else-
/here in France.

rance's Country ode	☎33
nternational Access ode	☎00
mbulance	☎15
olice	☎17
ire	☎18

Money

TMs

TMs are located at
he airport, the train
tation and on every
econd street corner.
isa, MasterCard
nd Amex are widely
ccepted.

Cash

ou always get a better
xchange rate in-
ountry but it is a good
dea to arrive
n Bordeaux with
nough euros to take
taxi to a hotel if you
ave to.

Money-Saving Tips

o Visit free museums and monuments such
as Bordeaux cathedral, place de la Bourse, Le
Garage Moderne and Basilique St-Seurin.

o Buy a Bordeaux Métropole City Pass (p23) –
arrive before noon at La Cité du Vin to take
advantage of the free admission included in
the pass.

o Scoot around town on foot or bicycle.

o Time your visit with the 1st Sunday of the
month when many sights are free.

Changing Money

o Commercial banks
charge up to €5 per
foreign-currency trans-
action – if they even
bother to offer exchange
services any more.

o Bureaux de change
(exchange bureaus) are
faster and easier, open
longer hours and often
give better rates than
banks.

o Some post-office
branches exchange
travellers cheques and
banknotes in a variety of
currencies but charge
a commission for cash;
most won't take US$100
bills.

Credit Cards

o Credit and debit cards
are accepted in most
places.

o French credit cards
have embedded chips –
you have to type in a PIN
to make a purchase.

o Visa, MasterCard and
Amex can be used in
shops and supermar-
kets and for train travel,
car hire and motorway
tolls.

o Don't assume that
you can pay for a meal
or a budget hotel with
a credit card – enquire
first.

Tipping

Restaurant and bar
prices already include
a 15% service charge;
if you were happy
with the service show
your appreciation by
leaving a small 'extra'
tip for your waiter or
waitress.

Dos & Don'ts

Conversation Use the formal *vous* when speaking to anyone unknown or older than you; the informal *tu* is reserved for close friends, family and children.

Churches Dress modestly (cover shoulders).

Drinks Asking for *une carafe d'eau* (free jug of tap water) in restaurants is acceptable. Never end a meal with a cappuccino or cup of tea. Play French and order *un café* (espresso).

French kissing Exchange *bisous* (cheek-skimming kisses) – two is the norm in Bordeaux – with casual acquaintances and friends.

Bars No tips for drinks served at bar; round to nearest euro for drinks served at table should service be exceptional.

Cafes Leave 5% to 10% for outstanding service, but absolutely no obligation.

Hotels Give porters €1 to €2 per bag.

Restaurants Leave 10% or a few euro coins on the table after paying the bill.

Tour guides Give €1 to €2 per person.

Public Holidays

New Year's Day (Jour de l'An) 1 January

Easter Sunday & Monday (Pâques & Lundi de Pâques) Late March/April

May Day (Fête du Travail) 1 May

Victoire 1945 8 May

Ascension Thursday (Ascension) May; on the 40th day after Easter

Pentecost/Whit Sunday & Whit Monday (Pentecôte & Lundi de Pentecôte) Mid-May to mid-June; on the seventh Sunday after Easter

Bastille Day/National Day (Fête Nationale) 14 July

Assumption Day (Assomption) 15 August

All Saints' Day (Toussaint) 1 November

Remembrance Day (L'onze Novembre) 11 November

Christmas (Noël) 25 December

Safe Travel

Bordeaux is a fairly safe city, but you should employ common sense.

o Avoid wandering alone at night in the Gare St-Jean, Marché des Capucins and place de la Victoire areas. None of these areas are dangerous, but they can attract shady characters and feel unsavoury after dark.

o Avoid walking anywhere near the Rive Garonne when drunk or unsteady on your feet; people drown in the river every year.

o Unless you absolutely have to, ditch the car. This is France's sixth largest city and parking, predictably, is a nightmare.

o Watch for pickpockets at the train station, Marche des Capucins and other busy tourist areas.

Smoking

o Ilegal in all indoor public spaces, including restaurants and pubs (though, of course, smokers still light up on the terraces outside).

Telephone

Calling France from abroad Dial your country's international access code, then 🕿 33 (France's country code), then the 10-digit local number without the initial zero.

Calling internationally from France Dial 🕿 00 (the international access code), the *indicatif* (country code), the area code (without the initial zero if there is one) and the local number. Some country codes are posted in public telephones.

Directory inquiries For *service national des renseignements* (directory inquiries) dial 🕿 11 87 12 or use the service for free online at www.118712.fr.

International directory inquiries For numbers outside France, dial 🕿 11 87 00.

Mobile Phones

o French mobile phone numbers begin with 06 or 07.

o France uses GSM 900/1800, which is compatible with Europe and Australia but not with the North American GSM 1900 or the totally different system in Japan (though some North Americans have tri-band phones that work here).

o Check with your service provider about roaming charges – dialling a mobile phone from a fixed-line phone or another mobile can be incredibly expensive.

o It is usually cheaper to buy a local SIM card from a French provider such as Orange, SFR, Bouygues Télécom or Free, which gives you a local phone number. Top up with prepaid credit, though this is likely to run out fast as domestic prepaid calls cost about €0.50 per minute.

o Recharge cards are sold at most *tabacs* (tobacconist-newsagents), supermarkets and online through websites such as Topengo (www.topengo.fr) or Sim-OK (https://recharge.sim-ok.com).

Toilets

o The French are completely blasé about unisex toilets, so save your blushes when tiptoeing past the urinals to reach the ladies' loo.

Charging Devices

Carrying your own charger and cable is the only sure way of ensuring you don't run out of juice. Don't be shy to ask in cafes and restaurants if you can plug in and charge – if you ask nicely, most will oblige. In Bordeaux the occasional cafe lends cables to customers and savvy taxi drivers stock a selection of smartphone-compatible cables and chargers for passengers to use.

○ No dawdling in mechanical, self-cleaning street toilets: you have precisely 15 minutes. Green means *libre* (vacant) and red means *occupé* (occupied).

Tourist Information

Tourist Office (Map p54, C2; ☎ 05 56 00 66 00; www.bordeaux-tourisme. com; 12 cours du 30 Juillet; ⊙9am-6.30pm Mon-Sat, to 5pm Sun) Runs an excellent range of city and regional tours; reserve in advance online or in situ. It also rents pocket modems to hook you up with wi-fi. There's a small but helpful **branch** (Map p80, F6; ☎ 05 56 00 66 00; rue Charles Domercq, Espace Modalis, Parvis Sud; ⊙9.30am-12.30pm & 2-6pm Mon-Fri) at the train station.

Maison du Tourisme de la Gironde (Map p54, B1; ☎ 05 56 52 61 40; www.gironde-tourisme.fr; 9 rue Fondaudège; ⊙9am-6pm Mon-Fri, 10am-1pm & 2-6.30pm Sat) Information on the surrounding Gironde *département*.

Visas

○ Generally not required for stays of up to 90 days (or at all for EU nationals); some nationalities need a Schengen visa.

○ For up-to-date details on visa requirements, see the website of the **Ministère des Affaires Étrangères** (Ministry of Foreign Affairs; www. diplomatie.gouv.fr; 37 quai d'Orsay, 7e; Ⓜ Assemblée Nationale) and click 'Coming to France'.

Responsible Travel

Support Local

○ Support initiatives that give back to the community: solidarity cafe **Wanted** (2 rue des Douves) near the Capucins market distributes 50 meals to the homeless each day and donates 2% of its turnover to Bordelais charities. Watch for a second Wanted to open in Rado at Bassins à Flot.

○ Volunteer with locals: the city's numerous *jardins partagés* (communal gardens) always welcome a helping hand. For Bordeaux associations seeking volunteers see https://associations bordeaux.fr.

○ Plug into what's happening on the ground with **Wanted Community**, a Facebook community of mutual aid and good-hearted sharing (buy, sell, share, ask for advice, advertise jobs etc) originating in Bordeaux.

Leave a Light Footprint

○ Public bike-sharing scheme **V3** is run by local public transport company TBM. Register online or with your credit card at a V3 station.

○ **Zoov** (www.zoov.eu) offer electric bikes for public sharing.

○ Download the app to locate and unlock a dock-less kick scooter (*trottinette*) from **Yego** (www.rideyego.com/ bordeaux), **Pony** (www. getapony.com/en) or **Dott** (www.ridedott.com).

Language

The sounds used in spoken French can almost all be found in English. There are a couple of exceptions: nasal vowels (represented in our pronunciation guides by 'o' or 'u' followed by an almost inaudible nasal consonant sound 'm', 'n' or 'ng'), the funny u sound ('ew' in our guides) and the deep-in-the-throat r. Bearing these few points in mind and reading our pronunciation guides below as if they were English, you'll be understood just fine. The markers (m) and (f) indicate the forms for male and female speakers.

To enhance your trip with a phrasebook, visit **lonelyplanet.com**.

Basics

Hello.
Bonjour.   bon·zhoor

Goodbye.
Au revoir.   o·rer·vwa

How are you?
*Comment   ko·mon
allez-vous?*   ta·lay·voo

I'm fine, thanks.
Bien, merci.   byun mair·see

Please.
S'il vous plaît. seel voo play

Thank you.
Merci.   mair·see

Excuse me.
Excusez-moi.   ek·skew·zay·mwa

Sorry.
Pardon.   par·don

Yes./No.
Oui./Non.   wee/non

I don't understand.
*Je ne comprends   zher ner kom·pron
pas.*   pa

Do you speak English?
*Parlez-vous   par·lay·voo
anglais?*   ong·glay

Eating & Drinking

..., please.
..., s'il vous plaît.   ... seel voo play

A coffee	*un café*	un ka·fay
A table for two	*une table pour deux*	ewn ta·bler poor der
Two beers	*deux bières*	der bee·yair

I'm a vegetarian.
*Je suis   zher swee
végétarien/   vay·zhay·ta·ryun/
végétarienne. (m/f)* vay·zhay·ta·ryen

That was delicious!
*C'était   say·tay
délicieux!*   day·lee·syer

The bill, please.
*L'addition,   la·dee·syon
s'il vous plaît.* seel voo play

Shopping

I'd like to buy ...
*Je voudrais   zher voo·dray
acheter ...*   ash·tay ...

I'm just looking.
Je regarde.   zher rer·gard

How much is it?
C'est combien?   say kom·byun

It's too expensive.
C'est trop cher. say tro shair

Can you lower the price?
Vous pouvez bay·say baisser le prix? — voo poo·vay / ler pree

Emergencies

Help!
Au secours! — o skoor

Call the police!
Appelez la police! — a·play la po·lees

Call a doctor!
Appelez un médecin! — a·play un mayd·sun

I'm sick.
Je suis malade. — zher swee ma·lad

I'm lost.
Je suis perdu/perdue. (m/f) — zher swee pair·dew

Where are the toilets?
Où sont les toilettes? — oo son lay twa·let

Time & Numbers

What time is it?
Quelle heure est-il? — kel er ay til

It's (eight) o'clock.
Il est (huit) heures. — il ay (weet) er

It's half past (10).
Il est (dix) heures et demie. — il ay (deez) er ay day·mee

morning	matin	ma·tun
afternoon	après-midi	a·pray·mee·dee
evening	soir	swar
yesterday	hier	yair
today	aujourd'hui	o·zhoor·dwee
tomorrow	demain	der·mun

Monday	lundi	lun·dee
Tuesday	mardi	mar·dee
Wednesday	mercredi	mair·krer·de
Thursday	jeudi	zher·dee
Friday	vendredi	von·drer·de
Saturday	samedi	sam·dee
Sunday	dimanche	dee·monsh

1	un	un
2	deux	der
3	trois	trwa
4	quatre	ka·trer
5	cinq	sungk
6	six	sees
7	sept	set
8	huit	weet
9	neuf	nerf
10	dix	dees
100	cent	son
1000	mille	meel

Transport & Directions

Where's ...?
Où est ...? — oo ay ...

What's the address?
Quelle est l'adresse? — kel ay la·dres

Can you show me (on the map)?
Pouvez-vous m'indiquer (sur la carte)? — poo·vay·voo mun·dee·kay (sewr la kart)

I want to go to ...
Je voudrais aller à ... — zher voo·dray a·lay a ...

Does it stop at (Amboise)?
Est-ce qu'il s'arrête à (Amboise)? — es·kil sa·ret a (om·bwaz)

I want to get off here.
Je veux descendre ici. — zher ver day·son·drer ee·see

Behind the Scenes

Send Us Your Feedback

We love to hear from travellers – your comments help make our books better. We read every word, and we guarantee that your feedback goes straight to the authors. Visit **lonelyplanet.com/contact** to submit your updates and suggestions.

Note: We may edit, reproduce and incorporate your comments in Lonely Planet products such as guidebooks, websites and digital products, so let us know if you don't want your comments reproduced or your name acknowledged. For a copy of our privacy policy visit lonelyplanet.com/privacy.

Acknowledgements

Cover photographs: (front) Miroir d'Eau, Bordeaux, Melanie Lemahieu/Shutterstock ©; (back) Canelés, Bordeaux's signature cake, Piotr Krzeslak/Shutterstock ©

Photographs pp36–7 (from left): Ivo Antonie de Rooij, Alvaro German Vilela, RossHelen, trabantos/Shutterstock ©

Nicola's Thanks

Heartfelt *bisous* to the many friends and professionals who aided and abetted in tracking down the best in Bordeaux, including Pauline Versace (La Cité du Vin), Emmeline Azra (St-Émilion) and Alexia Guelte. Kudos to my ever-fabulous co-writers and my ever-faithful, trilingual *France en famille* research team, Matthias, Niko, Mischa and Kaya Luefkens.

This Book

This 2nd edition of Lonely Planet's *Pocket Bordeaux* guidebook was researched, written and curated by Nicola Williams, as was the 1st. This guidebook was produced by the following:

Destination Editor
Daniel Fahey

Senior Product Editors
Daniel Bolger, Genna Patterson

Senior Cartographer
Mark Griffiths

Product Editors Kirsten Rawlings, Kate Mathews

Book Designers
Lauren Egan, Fergal Condon

Assisting Editors Melanie Dankel, Gabrielle Innes

Cartographers Rachel Imeson, Diana Von Holdt

Cover Researcher
Fergal Condon

Index

See also separate subindexes for:

🍴 Eating p157
🍷 Drinking p157
🎭 Entertainment p157
🛍 Shopping p157

Our Writer

Nicola Williams

Border-hopping is a way of life for British writer, runner, foodie, art aficionado and mum of three, Nicola Williams. Nicola has authored more than 50 guidebooks for Lonely Planet, and covers France as a destination expert for the *Telegraph*. She also writes for the *Independent,* the *Guardian,* lonelyplanet.com, *French Magazine, Cool Camping France* and others. Catch her on Twitter and Instagram @tripalong.

Published by Lonely Planet Global Limited
CRN 554153
2nd edition – Jun 2022
ISBN 978 1 78868 088 2
© Lonely Planet 2022 Photographs © as indicated 2022
10 9 8 7 6 5 4 3 2 1
Printed in Singapore